Be Your Own Beautiful

Be Your Own
Beautiful

Beauty in it's rarest form

Devin Brown

authorHOUSE®

AuthorHouse™
1663 Liberty Drive
Bloomington, IN 47403
www.authorhouse.com
Phone: 1-800-839-8640

Book cover and Photos done by Eric McGill
Make-up done by Destiny McGill
Blu' Suede Photography

Published by AuthorHouse   02/20/2013

ISBN: 978-1-4817-1658-1 (sc)
ISBN: 978-1-4817-1657-4 (e)

Library of Congress Control Number: 2013902907

Any people depicted in stock imagery provided by Thinkstock are models, and such images are being used for illustrative purposes only.
Certain stock imagery © Thinkstock.

This book is printed on acid-free paper.

Dedication

I dedicate this book to my loving grandmother, my best friend, Mary D. Jackson. To my mother, Karen Brown. And finally to my sisters, Raetequa Brown and Aundrea Brown:

Contents

Foreword ix

Introduction xi

Laying the Foundation 1

Finding the Roots 5

Who am I? 9

Self-Love 12

The Word No 15

Not Daddy's Little Girl 17

Friends (There Is Good in Good-bye) 21

Forgiveness 24

S.W.A.G. (Single While Awaiting God) 26

Rare Beauties (My Single Babies) 38

Rare Beauties Guidelines/Letter 39

Health 40

Goals 42

B.Y.O.B. (Be Your Own Beautiful) 44

B.Y.O.B. Interviews 49

Rare Beauties 136

Dedication 139

Acknowledgements 141

Giving Back 146

Foreword

As a Pastor and Bishop, I have seen the profound harmful effect on young girls, teens, and adults who have not learned their own value and worth.

It has been confirmed in study after study that there is a direct link between females having low self-esteem and those who marry too early, have babies out of wedlock, tolerate physical and emotional abuse, etc . . . . Lack of self-love is a common denominator in most every case. That's why I recommend females of all ages, read this book and hope parents, family members, and friends of girls of every age would get this book in their hands. It has the potential to help them navigate around and through the universal mistake of looking for love and validation in all the wrong places.

I applaud Devin for having the foresight, courage, and discipline to write a book on a very important subject. I have had the honor to be her pastor and have seen her evolve and mature into a beautiful young lady who has discovered her own beauty.

Bishop Porter L. Perry

Introduction

If you have my book, then you know that there has come a time for change in your life. A personal checkup is what I like to call it, and basically it's time to put things back into the right perspective. My prayer is that by the time you finish reading this book, you will not only have completed your personal checkup but that you will have also begun to deal with the things in your life and past to finally shatter the chains that have held you captive, breaking out of your cocoon to finally embrace "your own kind of beautiful!" Enjoy your journey, my Rare Beauties, and I will meet you at the finish line.

Laying the Foundation

One thing that I have found out about a lot of people, especially women and young ladies, is that we are scared to not only find out who we are, but we are also afraid to embrace our true selves once we discover the truth. Have you ever known someone who never stays by herself, every time you look around she has a new boyfriend or a new "best" friend? How about the person who is always seeking someone else's approval or duplicating what someone else's doing? If you have answered yes to these questions about someone you know, or even about yourself (if being honest), then you have just identified some of the key signs of an individual who, sadly, does not know who they are and has yet to discovered their worth.

I was there once! The person who I just described was me just a few years ago. I had to sit myself down and pray to God; I remember feeling so alone, just like it was yesterday. I remember so many times where I would be in a room full of people, even family and friends, hanging out, yet I still felt like I was the only person there. During this time I found myself handling everyone else's problems except my own. Thinking back, I now realize that it was my excuse for placing my own problems on the back burner rather than having to face them. I began to pray for peace of mind, because I was dying slowly. Not a physical death, but an emotional death. The person I was inside, that rare beauty that was buried deep within me that I had not yet met, was also dying; therefore, I prayed for an emotional resurrection.

You see, there is a real danger when you don't know who you are; you become an easy target, making it possible for anyone to mold you into becoming who "they" think you should be. Then, before you know it, you find yourself living a life that does not belong to you, constantly searching for happiness that can never be found because the life you are living is not your own, so you really can't know what form of happiness you need. Your life becomes a smoke screen and even you are deceived by the façade that's in place. But you can't discover your true self because you have no clue who you are. How do I know? I know because that is exactly where I found myself and that's what's happening to a lot of you, as well.

I want you to know that there is a way out, and although this will not be an easy process, it is a very achievable goal and well worth it. I want this so much for you, but I can't desire this more than you. So I pose these three questions to you and it is my prayer that by the time you've finished this book that you are able to answer them.

1. Am I ready to be honest with myself?
2. Am I ready for change?
3. Am I ready to embrace the beauty that is uniquely mine?

Hopefully you have answered yes to all three questions and if you have, then you have just begun to shatter your chains and break free, which is all we need in order to proceed to a better you!

You may be wondering what it means to be your own beautiful, so let me explain:

Webster describes "own" as "belonging to; belonging exclusively or especially to; peculiar; to hold as property; to have a legal or rightful title to; to be the proprietor or possessor of; to possess," and "kind" is described as "a category of things distinguished by some common characteristic or quality." So when I speak of being your own beautiful, I am referring to the beauty that is uniquely yours. It is up to *you* to realize that God designed you with customized characteristics and qualities that distinguish you from others. When I picture you, I picture someone remarkably rare. Someone unusual and uncommon, someone special in the purest form, and yes, someone exceptionally beautiful. So as you read my words, I need you to realize that you are someone more than average and far from common; someone who is beautiful in the simplest form. And when I researched the word beauty, Webster states it as "the qualities that give pleasure to the senses," which means it gives pleasure to all our senses—vision, hearing, touch, taste, and smell. That means everything about you from the inside out should be pleasurable. Beauty also is described as a "deep satisfaction to the mind," which I love because it proves that beauty is not just something on the outside or outer appearance, but it is essentially something that has to develop on the inside first, which develops your character.

So from now on I will refer to you as my Rare Beauties; you are your own kind of beautiful. Yes, everyone is different in their own way and that's what makes us unique and exceptionally beautiful. Just like a fragrance, your qualities and characteristics are your own personal stamp to be burnished in the minds and hearts of those you encounter. Those are the things that set you apart.

Have you ever met someone and your first thought of that person was "Oh, she is beautiful" (by an outer appearance standard), but as soon as she opened her mouth and revealed what was on the inside, your entire opinion of her being "beautiful" changed?

What about that person who was not, in your opinion, "good-looking" according to what the norms of our society dictate, but once you got a chance to know them there was something so vibrant about them that their whole outer image became beautiful? You know that saying beauty is in the eye of the beholder? Everyone has their belief about you and what is beautiful to them, and that is okay since we are all entitled to our own ideas.

So let's take it a little further. For instance, I had to learn not to prejudge people before I got the chance to know them. In life, we have to learn not to prejudge people and should instead get to know a person's qualities and character beforehand. I admit that I, too, have been guilty of this in the past. I would meet someone and would have already judged them based on their outer appearance (hair, clothes, makeup, etc.). The older and wiser I became and as God began to work on me from the inside out, I have realized that beauty really lies within. You should always want someone in your life that can help propel you to where you need to be, or someone who keeps you steady on the path you are on (as long as it's the right path—don't forget you want to be sure you are not walking down someone else's road). You don't want anyone that will pull you down. I have found out a lot of ladies have what I like to call the "crab syndrome." For instance, if you put a whole bunch of crabs in one bucket they will all try to get to the top, but none of them ever will because there is always a crab pulling the other one down. We will get to that a little later in the book and explain how it relates to us as women. Hopefully those who are reading this that may possess that characteristic will be able to take that garment off and no longer operate this way.

So, my Rare Beauties, now that I have laid the foundation of this book, let's get started. I'm so excited . . . how about you?

Finding the Roots

For me, the journey began at birth and considering that I was born prematurely, maybe even inside my mother's womb; I believe that from the start, God had a destined plan for me and my life. Pregnant at fifteen, my mother gave birth to me two months early. Therefore, even from birth I had to fight extra hard to be here, being that I only weighed two pounds and fifteen ounces; I know, small, huh? During this time, it was a struggle for my mother because she had a newborn and no place to stay. She and her siblings were split up because her mother—my grandmother, whom I loved dearly—was battling a drug addiction that left her unable to see past the haze of chemical-induced utopia. Therefore, my mom was forced to fend for the both of us . . . alone.

Growing up, I don't ever remember there being a time where I saw my mother cry or complain over what she could or could not do for us. This experience left my sisters and me very thankful for the little that we did have. My mother was a single parent of three girls, with me being the oldest. By the time I was in the second grade I began to feel as though it was time to grow up and help my mother as much as I possibly could. Now, my mother never asked me to do this, it was just something I felt I needed to do because even as a child, it hurt my heart to see her constantly tired, yet always trying to do it all herself. I would do little things around the house for my mom; I remember her pulling up a kitchen chair to the sink and allowing me to wash the plates, bowls, cups, and silverware while she took care of the knives and pots. I enjoyed this time because I felt I was doing all I could to help her.

I began to feel as if I were the "other adult" in the house. I mean, why not? I had taken on the responsibility of helping out around the house with cleaning, cooking, watching my little sisters, and whatever else needed to be done. As time went on with me being the other grown-up, it also caused my mother and me to start bumping heads. My attitude spiraled out of control because realistically I was way too young to deal with the pressure and stress. Finally it had gotten so bad (my attitude, that is) that when my mother would leave to go out with her friends, I would stay up waiting for her because I was so anxious. I worried about things that I should not have been concerned about as a child. I would wait and wait and when I couldn't stay up any longer, I would write her angry notes that said "I hate you," and because we didn't have tape I would lick the back of the paper and stick them on the wall.

Little did I know that my mom was under just as much stress and pressure as I was. Soon she would try to find a temporary escape by going out and partying with friends, and I remember I couldn't wait till the next morning to see if she had read my notes. I can vividly recall waking up early in the morning to see if my mother had acknowledged the notes or not and, to my surprise, they were still there. They had not been moved—not one bit. My feelings were so hurt because what I really desired was for her to wake me out of my sleep, hold me, and talk to me about this anger and bitterness toward her that had consumed me, but she never did. I remember asking her later on that day if she had seen and read my notes and she replied yes. That was all . . . she never said another word about it.

Now I'm not saying that my mother didn't care, because I know she did, without a doubt.

Now that I am older, I have come to realize that it was extremely hard for my mother to be the type of parent that I felt she should have been and wanted her to be, because she hadn't had her own mother in her life as an example to teach her how to be loved and show it through her actions.

She didn't know how; all she knew was how to survive. My mother had been forced to live her life in survival mode and since she'd had no one there to hold and comfort her, she didn't know how to give and show her emotional side, that side of her that I so desperately desired and yearned for. She didn't want her children to struggle or have to wonder where we were going to lay our heads or where we were going to get our next meal.

Devin Brown

She had vowed to herself that her children would never end up homeless and hungry like she had when she was a child, so even though she was young and single, she did the best she could for us.

By the time I was in middle school, I became "the woman" of the house (at least in my mind). My mother worked an overnight job driving buses, so I ended up running the household. I would cook full-course meals, and although it was far from perfect, I would do the best that I could to make sure my "children" (my sisters) were fed. By this time my anger was so out of control that it was now not only toward my mother but anyone and everyone who would cross my path. Because I liked school I didn't fight at school; I would wait until I got home to take my anger and frustrations out on my sisters. I was a very mean girl, to the point that I would literally fight my sisters over any little thing!

Now let's pause right here, because I know I'm not the only person who has been through this, and I'm sure many of you have been through much worse.

So the first step toward "finding the root" is getting to know who you are, and even though it may seem hard, it's really not. You just have to sit yourself down and think. You may want a pen or pencil to write down your thoughts, and that's okay. Think back on your past as far back as you can remember and find out where it all began, because that is the root where you will need to begin the cutting and pruning. Just like a tree or plant, if you only cut its limbs here and there, it's going to keep growing back and when it does, it will come back thicker than before and soon will begin to block out your sight of that beautiful image waiting to be seen (the real you). Instead of just pruning sporadically, start with the most permanent solution, which is to remove it, and you do that by cutting it down at the root. In order to begin the process of becoming a better you, you have to get to the root of the matter for it to be gone for good.

So that's what I had to do—for me the root of my hatred toward my mother was due to her lack of love and affection toward me. By it not being dealt with, I developed a false sense of balance, never knowing the difference between staying in my place as a child and feeling as though

I needed to be an adult to help my mom. It wasn't until I discovered the "root" that I was able to understand that I had taken it upon myself to be the "other adult" and "the woman of the house," therefore planting the seeds that grew into what would later become the root of my self-imposed problems. In all honesty, my mother never asked me to assume those roles and responsibilities . . . but because I created those roots, I realized that it was me who had to destroy them.

Who am I?

By the time I entered high school, my grandmother had passed away. I began to gain weight, going quickly from 140 pounds to two hundred pounds due to my grandmother's passing; I ended up losing a huge part of my mother also, which caused me to begin taking full responsibility around the house with the exception of paying the bills. I was going to school, cooking, cleaning, working, taking care of my sisters—"my kids"—and my mother. My mother and grandmother were very close, so when she died, my mother fell into a deep depression. Although grandmother battled a drug addiction, it didn't stop her children and grandchildren from loving her. It was almost as if we were trying to love her out of her condition. My grandmother would leave for entire weekends, and each time we would welcome her back with open arms. In the midst of this, she became my mom's best friend, someone for my mother to talk to and someone for my mother to get advice from. She would even help Mother around Christmastime for us. My grandmother became the mediator between me and my mother; I can't even begin to tell you how many calls she received from us. Not only was she my mother's best friend, she also became mine. God delivered her from her drug addiction years before she passed and saved her soul. She ended up dying from having too much potassium at the age of fifty. My mother was heartbroken, which caused her deep depression, and as I stated before, she would barely eat, she didn't work, and once again she wasn't there to give my sisters and me the attention that we needed. So I continued to pick up the slack where she couldn't. I got so busy with doing for others that I forgot about me—it seemed as though everyone forgot about me. I was angrier than before and I began to take it out on my friends, trying to boss them around like they were my kids, and if they didn't listen then it was a problem, a big problem. On the outside no one noticed that I was a troubled girl, but on the inside I was torn to pieces. The craziest part of it all was that this way of life had become so familiar to me that I didn't really think anything was wrong; I thought this was "normal"—I was just being me!

If you were to ask me back then "Devin, who are you," I would have had to return the question—who am I? I didn't know! I had no clue who I was nor did I know what I enjoyed doing. Usually kids in high school are playing sports or are on a school committee, but I didn't have time for that because I had to be there for my "kids" and my mother. I felt it was my responsibility to make sure they were all okay and taken care of, even if I wasn't, because I felt I had to be strong for them. If you ask me now, I would say I felt like I was robbed of my childhood and I wasn't given the opportunity to have one, therefore I was not able to get to enjoy the things in life as a child. My mind was always on grown-up things like *what are we going to eat tonight?* One of my aunts would tell me "you shouldn't be worried about these things; you need to be a child," then she would say I was going to look old before my time. My response would always be *how do you become a child?* I was so confused—I felt like if I didn't do these things then they were not going to be done, and in my mind my sisters counted on me and I couldn't let them down.

I ended up graduating from high school like I promised my grandmother I would. I was the first person in my family to do so and that alone was a big triumph. The bigger achievement was me graduating without having any children. So not only was my family proud of me, for the first time I was proud of me! Now don't get me wrong—I know some of you reading this may already be parents and you're still in school, but remember, this is my personal story and it's not meant to make any of you feel bad but only to help you see that no matter what the state of affairs is, you can still be more than what circumstances dictate.

So, my Rare Beauties, my question to you is *who are you?*

You might not be able to respond to this now, but my prayer is that by the time you get to the end of this book and you have completed all the questions, you will have an idea of who you are, so begin to start asking yourself this.

Devin Brown

Note to parents: let's be careful how we handle our children, especially the oldest. For instance, if you have another baby, your initial goal is not to make your first child feel left out. We start out by letting them feel special by going to get diapers or throwing them away. Then it turns into making them feel as if they have to do it, instead of feeling like they are a help and giving them a choice to want to do it. Demands quickly follow, like go get your sister or brother or making them feel bad for not watching their sibling. Remember, let them be a child and allow them to have their childhood. As a parent, the responsibilities are yours, not your other children's. Please don't get me wrong in any way—it's good to raise your children to know how to be accountable; however, in teaching your children duties at an earlier age, make sure you're not crossing that fine line and teaching them to be responsible by making them feel obligated to take care of your own tasks.

Self-Love

Happiness comes from focusing on what you really what to do; the hard part is finding the strength to actually do it.

By the time my sisters and I became adults, they had begun to do their own thing and march to the beat of their own drum, leaving me lost and still butting into their business and trying to run their lives. This was something they clearly didn't want me to do anymore and it began to drive a wedge between us. I can still hear them say to me "you're not our mama; you're our big sister!" This would hurt my feelings so badly I would think to myself *what happened?* All I was trying to do was help and I felt as if I were no longer needed, which left me feeling even more lost than before. If you remember me saying early on about always handling everyone else's problems but my own, it was honestly an escape from my own issues. I always had to be in someone else's business, trying to solve their tribulations, feeling as though I was a very good friend. What got lost in translation was that I figured if I focused on others, then I never had to look in the mirror at *myself.*

I finally came to a place in my life where I began to think and ask myself the question *Who am I?* and what are my passions in life, what is my purpose, what is my destiny and what makes me the happiest? These were very hard questions to answer because I thought I loved me, but I quickly realized that I didn't, and I didn't know how to, either. The time came for me to find myself. In spite of the grief my mother was dealing with due to the loss of her mother, I realized if I was going to be any good for her or anyone else, I first had to learn how to be good to myself, so I began to ask myself these questions:

What makes me happy?
What do I like to do?

What do I like to do in my "me" time?
Most of all who am I?

Now the thing that I loved to do the most was to go to church. I loved God and honestly He was holding me up during this entire time and even though I didn't see it then, I know it now. I also loved to read the Bible and fictional books. Now I know this might sound strange, but reading for me was like a vacation because it allowed me to get away and I could read for hours a day. At that time, those were the things that made me happy, but it also began to create another issue for me—I began to believe that since I was saved and going to church, if others were not getting their life together like me (i.e. going to church and being saved), then they were the devil. I know, crazy, huh? I had begun to judge people and didn't even realize I was doing it. People couldn't do anything around me: cuss, smoke, listen to secular music, or anything that I thought was a "sin." If they were going to be around me, they had to be what I believed in my mind was "holier than thou." It took God speaking to my heart to realize that this was not how God intended for me to reach out to people. God didn't treat me that way when I was in my mess; he loved me out of it. I realized that I still had a lot to learn about salvation and what it really meant to live for Christ, because it wasn't about an outer appearance at all, and this was something I had to come to terms with rapidly!

As time went on I began to hang out with friends and I started to find out what it was I really liked to do (and I'm still learning these things as I grow). I love to travel, and even though I hadn't traveled much, I did get the opportunity to visit a friend from middle school who lives in Denver, Colorado. It amazes me that through it all, through my faults and mistakes and all that I had taken her through, she still remained my friend—now that is a testimony all by itself! I was able to see a world outside of Texas and realized that there was so much more I had to learn. That trip ignited something within me and I made a vow to myself to make sure I traveled every year for the rest of my life. I established that I enjoyed going to the movies; it has a calming effect on me. I also have a bit of a competitive nature, which came about when I discovered my love for bowling (mind you, I'm not a good bowler at all). However, I love the time I get to spend with family and friends when we get together to go bowling. During my free time, I still love to read or just sit by the water listening to music and thinking.

So, my Rare Beauties, I want you to take out a notebook and begin to write those questions down and do your best to answer them. Then I want you to make the effort to experience them and live them. I want you to know that change is a good thing, though it may seem scary at first—trust me I know! Anything that is out of the norm is always going to seem scary at first. Once you make the decision to not live your life in fear and begin to embrace who you really are, you are going to see things in your life take on an entirely new meaning and you will find yourself finally on your path of discovering your true purpose. Everything in life is about choices, so you should always choose to love yourself the way God intended for you to be loved.

The things that I have shared with you I did by myself. Yes, I went to the movies by myself all the time; I had to get to know who I was. The greatest thing about this is that because I have spent so much time by myself, when I got around others and I did something that was ugly or mean, it immediately caught my attention. I had to tell myself *no*, this was not acceptable anymore and I have to change—you should always treat others the way you want to be treated. It was hard at first because I was so used to being mean all the time, but I quickly realized that it took way more energy to be mean than it took to just be nice. Because I really wanted to change, I began to pray all the time, asking God to help me become the type of friend that I wanted for myself and the type of person I wanted to be associated with. Even to this very day, I make a conscious choice to be nice to people and treat people right! I had to start making better decisions and realized that if I couldn't stand to be by myself, then no one else would want to be with me, either. This was all in the process of learning to really love "me," because if I couldn't love me, then how could I expect anyone else to?

Devin Brown

The Word No

Okay, Rare Beauties, I know that this is hard for most of us to do. It was hard for me, and at times, it still is. At this point in my life I love myself, but I had another conflicting area in my life that I had to overcome. That area was the word *no*! How many of my Rare Beauties feel if they say no, no one is going to like them, or that they might hurt someone's feelings? Well, this was me, especially since I was trying to get out of being mean to people. This was really hard for me, and once again I prayed, and the revelation I got is that if God doesn't lay it on your heart to do, and you don't want to do it, then you don't have to. Now if He does, then that's what you need to find yourself doing, young or old. Remember, just because you got this eye-opener doesn't mean everyone else around you has, so yes, you may still get called mean or selfish sometimes, but that's okay!

Selfishness—let's talk about this. In my belief, there is a fine line between selfishness and wisdom, and it's up to you to know the difference. Someone may think you are being selfish when you choose to have some "me" time, but that is wisdom and balance. It is important that you have that (wisdom and balance), because if you are always being everything for everyone, when will you have time to be something for yourself? We all need time to regroup and love ourselves—we need time to get into the presence of God and allow him to restore us. This, Rare Beauties, is wisdom and balance, not selfishness.

Being the backbone of my family, I get called for everything. There was a time that whenever I would get a call, I would drop everything I was doing to save the person or the situation, to the point where I grew tired mentally, physically, and emotionally. God began to deal with me about this, and tell me "You are not God; I am. Your family is on loan to you. Give them back to me. You can't do what I can do for them,

Devin Brown

and that's why you're so tired all the time—you are operating outside of the capacity that I have given unto you." He was right! I told God out loud, "God you can have your job back." I gave him everything: my mother, sisters, nieces, nephew, friends, bills, and I gave him myself. And every time something came up or something crossed my mind because I worried too much, I had to remind myself that I had given it to God, and I would say, "God I gave you back your job, so you have to handle it," and I would leave it there. I still do this. Every day is a choice for me and you, my Rare Beauties; we should choose daily the path of positive change. You might feel alone at first, and that's okay, just remember that nothing worth having is easy. I truly believe that loving yourself, having a peaceful mind, and enjoying life is worth having, don't you?

One thing I have also learned to be true is that people will never grow if you don't let them learn from their own mistakes. Have you ever heard that saying a "hard head makes a soft behind?" Well if you are always running to someone's rescue, they will never hit rock bottom to feel how hard it is and that it hurts! Would you keep doing something that hurts? No! You learn from it. So if you are always there, like I was, then they will always have that cushion from you and you take the fall, you feel the pain that they should have felt, causing you to become mentally, physically, and emotionally drained.

Let me ask you this, my Rare Beauties, how can you love someone when you don't know how to love yourself?

How can you have a healthy relationship with anyone if you can't teach them how you want to be loved?

And honestly, how can you truly help someone when you haven't been helped yourself?

The answer is you can't, it's impossible.

So please remember when God has not pressed it upon your heart to do it, and you don't want to do it, then it's okay for the answer to be *no*! You are not obligated!

Devin Brown

Not Daddy's Little Girl

First off, I have to give a big thumbs-up to my mother and all the other mothers playing both parts; it's not easy.

My dad was not in my life growing up; I can remember very vaguely when I was young the times that he was there. From what I was told, I was his little girl, and I loved being around my daddy. There's a lot I don't know about what happened and why he left, but I know he had his own demons he was battling with, such as drugs. The things that I endured because of him not being in my life were hard, and I believe that I held a lot of hatred toward him as well. However, God had a lot of men in my life, such as my uncles, to play that part. To tell me how beautiful I am. To tell me I can do this, I can do that. If I called for advice, they were there to answer. So I will forever appreciate that.

I have come to the realization that a lot of young women are searching for that daddy type of love, but in the wrong ways. They are searching for it by being with different guys or being very promiscuous. I also understand that some young ladies have developed a trust issue when it comes to men; this can happen if your dad comes in and out of your life, not fulfilling his promises.

When I hear someone say they are "daddy's little girl," I think of someone that is very close to their father, someone that plays and watches sports with her father. I think how much her father tells her how beautiful she is and that she is his little princess. I think about how much he overshadows her with his love.

So with that being said, I am not "daddy's little girl"—I never had a father to tell me how much he loved me and that I was his princess. Just

Devin Brown

like so many of my Rare Beauties, I grew up without a father. My mother played both parts.

I believe that it is so important that both parents play their parts in raising a child, whether they are together or not. Another thing a (good) father does, in my opinion, is teach us as girls how a man should treat us. It's harder to pick that up from your mom, I think. But not impossible—I have seen it done.

It helps balance out that child's life. And even though my father was not in my life, my mother did a very good job on her own (my hat goes off to her).

But there were just some areas in my life that had voids to be filled. I was always looking for that love of a father but searching in the wrong places, and my heart was broken so many times.

I believe that a lot of young ladies (even grown women) who had that missing void filled it with so many hurtful things—men, drugs, and the pursuit of material things. These things can only make you feel well for a limited time. Even though I was not a promiscuous child, I still fell for every sweet nothing a guy whispered in my ear, just because it sounded good and I had never heard it before. If some of my Rare Beauties are being honest right now, you too will be agreeing with me. I believe that if my father had been in my life actively and told me how beautiful I was and taught me the mind games guys play (you know, the father and daughter talks) and had been there to have a conversation with a guy, I would have done a little better in my judgment of character when it came to men.

I know a lot of women cannot stand to be by themselves; they feel like they need that man in their life at all times whether he is good for them or not, just because they want to be loved. And they do whatever it takes to keep him, and their priorities are all messed up.

I believe God put people in our paths for a reason, so let's utilize them to help us get to our next level: some might be there for a season or a lifetime.

Devin Brown

I have tried to make peace with my father before now, and when it seemed to be going good, there I was, left with broken promises, just like every other man that has come into my life. I remember about a year and a half ago, I went to go and visit my father who was, at the time, in prison. I had just begun to love myself and wanted to make peace with him and start the forgiveness in my heart. When I got there, he was very shocked to see me; we sat down after I gave him a hug. I began to tell him that I really needed him consistently in my life. I told him I was no longer worried about the past and what had happened between him and my mother (that will come later—for some reason he always wanted to dwell on the past) but I wanted to concentrate on right now and the future and to see if it will actually hold something for us. I told him how I wanted to be loved as a daughter. You know what bothers me the most is that even though things didn't work out between him and my mother, that didn't mean that they couldn't work out between us.

I remember looking in my father's eyes and telling him the reason why he couldn't be a father was because he didn't know how! And his response as he stared right back at me was "You might be right!" I felt like that was the most honest thing he had ever said to me, and then he looked at me with tears in his eyes and asked me if we could start over. I actually felt like my trip was worth it, that my father and I could actually start a father-daughter relationship even though I was twenty-eight.

Since then my father has gotten out, and he actually is doing very well so far—he has been calling me almost every day. And we have been talking and laughing. I can appreciate this new start we have.

I wanted to put this chapter in here to first to let you know that you are not by yourselves. And that you do not have to settle for any guy that comes your way to feel loved or wanted. My advice is to find an uncle (like I did) or a good friend of the family that you can trust and look up to as a father figure. So, my Rare Beauties, you are not the only ones that have been fatherless. I have, too, and I thank God that I have turned out as well as I have. But I did want to talk about this just to let you ladies know it's time for us to start forgiving and pressing on. That is where I am right now. And don't let the fact that your father wasn't in your life be an excuse as to why you haven't succeeded in life or why you can't be respected when it comes to men.

Find it in your heart for forgiveness, even if the times that you approached your father didn't seem like they were worth it. In the end it really is about if you have made peace within yourself. My Rare Beauties, if he can't see what a priceless gem you are, it is definitely his loss, and that goes for any other guy in the world that doesn't have any admiration for the good woman you have become. He should acknowledge you and the love that you have for yourself. You are priceless, you are Rare, and you are Beautiful—**know it and own it**!

Friends
(There Is Good in Good-bye)

I thank God for changing me; I'm so grateful! When I finally learned how to love myself the way God intended, I was able to love others properly, as well. When God restored me, He took the anger away and replaced it with compassion. It's so funny, because now I cry about everything. It's the truth, and my family and friends are always laughing at me. All I can say is God has a sense of humor.

As far as friends go, I can count them on one hand—I have a very small circle and most of them I have known for over ten years. It is amazing that they have remained in my life even through all my rude and mean years, but through it all they have witnessed my growth and have not judged me and for that I am grateful! One of my friends once told me that a friendship is like a marriage: you have to consider the other person, which includes their feelings, and you should always treat them like you would want to be treated, both of you giving one hundred percent.

At this point I will advise that you take time and write down all your friends, acquaintances, and those who just truly don't mean you any good. Now your acquaintances could be people that you're just getting to know (but be careful, don't open up too much).

Who is a friend? A friend is someone who sticks closer than a brother.

I know you are probably thinking, "Blood is thicker than water!" But I will have to disagree, that's not always a truth in every relationship you have. In my past experiences I have found that after I bent over backward for some family members, even to the point of giving them my last, when I needed them they were nowhere to be found. When I have done the same thing for a friend they were always there to pick up the pieces. Now, I'm not saying this is true about every person you call friend or every family member, but as you continue to live and learn you will soon recognize the difference.

Do you have a "friend" that likes to argue all the time? News flash—that is not your friend, instead it is a very unhealthy relationship that you must get yourself out of; I was in that position on both sides. At one point in my life I was the one starting the arguing (because I was unhappy) and the other part I was receiving the abuse from someone else (because I did not love myself enough at the time to put a stop to it).

Now, let me stop here, my Rare Beauties. I love my friends; they are like sisters to me, but I started learning how to love myself, and I don't have time to entertain drama. I had to let everyone in my life know that I am no longer willing to go through any drama with them anymore, that I love myself enough to stop it before it ruins another friendship or relationship. I have learned that real communication is the key to keeping our relationships healthy.

Communicating, my Rare Beauties, is something else I want to talk to you about. Communication is very vital to who you are, If you can't talk about what's bothering you, it will eat you up. Communication is the foundation to every good and successful relationship. When I speak on relationships, that can mean any number of people: mother, father, sister, friend, or significant other. Every type of relationship needs a good foundation made up of God, communication, trust, and love. If you don't have these, then you have something that is built on sand and will not stand the test of time.

I was in a bad friendship at one point in my life and at the time I believed we were true friends, but somewhere down the line we lost it, and the friendship became very unhealthy and toxic for me. I pretty much let this individual define who I was. I always sought her approval on everything. If she didn't like what I was wearing, I took it off. If she said let's do it, you better believe I was doing it. But we argued all the time and I was so unhappy. I said earlier on that this was one of the qualities of not loving yourself—seeking approval of someone else.

Devin Brown

I was so dependent on her that if she was not around I was lost. But God helped me get out of this situation. Have you ever heard the saying "I prayed for God to deliver me from my enemies and I started losing friends?" Well, that's what happened here.

I got so sick and tired of being on her string and moving when she said to move. Now, let me say this: I don't blame her one bit; it was my fault and I blame myself because I allowed this to go on for nine years. However, I also must say that through this experience I grew, and I was able to see things about myself that I hadn't before and was able to change them!

My Rare Beauties, a note to self: A good sign that you have found and love yourself is when you no longer seek validation or approval from others.

The last thing I want to share with you in this chapter is something I mentioned earlier, and that's "The Crab Syndrome." This affects all people, but I have really noticed it in women—they hate to see you do well and become successful. The Crab Syndrome represents people pulling you down to get to the top. If you ever see a bushel of crabs in a bucket, they are always clawing at one another, trying to climb over each other to get to the top. In reality, this is how the world and society is today, which is sad because this syndrome causes *no one* to make it to the top.

You have to pay attention to your surroundings because this syndrome can come from your frienemies (people who act like your friends but then talk about you behind your back or are always putting you down).

Leave them alone—this is not healthy!

Forgiveness

My Rare Beauties, forgiveness is a very essential part of your growth, and it's imperative that you do this. Like with me and my mother, our relationship is so much better now. I no longer hate my mother—I love her. We still have our disagreements, but who doesn't? I do not hold the past against her and I do not bring it up to hurt her; this is true forgiveness. I have shared with my mother about my experience and my process of becoming a better me, my own beautiful. She has taken what I have shared and applied it to her life and by doing so she was able to beat depression. My mother is still on her course to find out who she is, but she doesn't have to do it alone, because I'm right by her side, helping along the way, loving her through it. God is so amazing. I remember one day my mother was hospitalized for her depression. I went to go see her and we shared a long-overdue talk where I began to talk to my mother about the "hate you" notes on the wall from my childhood. She told me she remembers them. I told my her how much I felt like she hurt me during me that time and how all I really wanted was for her to come and hold me and tell me everything was going to be okay. My mother apologized to me and it felt good, and I believe that the healing process for my mother and me began that day. I began to tell her that she needed to forgive my grandmother for everything that she had done to her in the past, to let it go. My mother lay in the hospital bed with tears in her eyes, and even though she didn't say anything, I know she heard me. I believe that she has let some things go and is still a work in progress, but so are we all.

Remember, my Rare Beauties, forgiveness is not only for the other person, but also for you! Also, it's not just about you forgiving someone who has hurt you, but about you also asking the ones you have hurt to forgive you, then forgiving yourself!

Devin Brown

I am not asking or suggesting you to do anything that I myself have not already done. For instance, I went to my sisters and asked for their forgiveness. I asked them to forgive me for all that I had put them through growing up, the abusive behavior and trying to run their life. I explained to them that I had been dealing with a lot and didn't know how to handle it, so I took it out on them. I also told them I would do my best to stay out of their affairs and allow them to live their own lives, though this would not be an easy task for me because I only want the best for them. I asked them to help me with this (it's okay to ask for help) and most of all I let them know that I loved them.

I did the same with my friends, asking for their forgiveness for me being so mean, and from having a know-it-all attitude and from the spirit of jealousy that took over my life for a while, causing me to not allow *my* friends to have any other friends but me, and they couldn't do anything with anyone else unless I was there. Yeah, I know what you're probably thinking, because even as I write this, I'm moved to tears at the thought that I was even like that—was that person really me? I'm so grateful that I have been delivered from that person and I'm even more grateful that in spite of my issues, my friends stayed by my side and are still a part of my life, and we have very healthy relationships now.

As I stated before, I also asked my mother for forgiveness. This was hard for me at that point in time because back then I didn't feel like I did anything wrong. Truth be told, instead of telling her how I felt as a child, I decided to write notes describing to her how much I hated her. That led to my disrespectful ways growing up as a teenager and even in my early adult life. I was wrong, and I came to terms with it, asked for forgiveness, and the healing process between my mother and me has been an amazing one!

My family and friends forgave me, I forgave myself, and most importantly, God forgave me.

S.W.A.G.
(Single While Awaiting God)

Having swag is very important!

In order for you to attract whatever it is that makes you happy in a mate, you have to make sure that you know what happy truly means to you. This won't be long, so I will just get straight to the point!

In order for you to attract whatever it is that makes you happy in a guy, you have to make sure that you know what happy truly means to you.

For me the foundation of a relationship is God, Communication, Friendship, and Trust.

Let's break this down:

God is love.

If you and your mate have God, He will truly teach you how to love one another unconditionally.

Communication—to convey information about; make known; impart and to reveal clearly; manifest.

I am a true believer of communicating. I don't like going around making assumptions about something or someone. The crazy thing is it tears you up on the inside, and the other person has no idea that you feel this way, and they go about life normally.

If you talk about (not argue) whatever is going on, it doesn't have time to set and become bitter or even turn into anger or hatred toward that person, or in this case the "opposite."

Friendship—Aristotle said, "What is a friend? A single soul, dwelling in two bodies."

Value that is found in friendships is often the result of a friend demonstrating the following on a consistent basis:

- The tendency to desire what is best for the other <u>person</u>
- Sympathy and empathy
- Honesty, perhaps in situations where it may be difficult for others to speak the truth, especially in terms of pointing out the perceived faults of one's counterpart
- Mutual understanding and compassion, ability to go to each other for emotional support
- Enjoyment of each other's company
- Trust in one another
- Positive reciprocity—a relationship is based on equal give and take between the two parties
- The ability to be oneself, express one's feelings, and make mistakes without fear of judgment

It is very important to have honesty, trust, sympathy, respect, and helpfulness in friendship.

I believe a lot of relationships fall by the wayside, and you see a lot of girls and women hopping from one guy to the next because we don't know who we are or know how to love ourselves as individuals, let alone how to make anyone else happy.

There's always going to be a lot of confusion going on from each party because you think that he should be doing this and that, because that's what you told him you wanted once before and when he finally does it, it's not what you desired! So he is confused, but what is it that you really want? Do you know? Let me answer that for you—*no*!

The thing is, you really don't know what you want because you haven't had time to know who you are and what it is you really like. Subconsciously, you're really just expecting someone to come and define who you are, and I honestly think you are asking way too much of that person.

Going into a relationship, you should be bringing something to it and not taking away from it.

Bring your whole, complete self. (Not saying you are going to be perfect—no one is.)

Have your own place, your own ride, and your own job—show independence.

Where do you place yourself?

I took a little survey from guys and asked these questions:

1. What is it that you look for in a woman?
2. What is it that turns you off about a woman?

These are the answers I got!

You will fit in one of three categories:

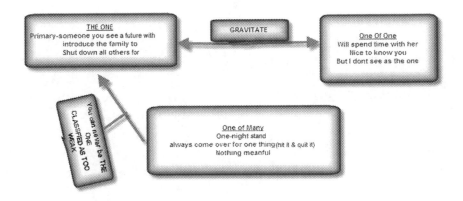

The Turn-ons:

1. Lovely shape and looks—A woman who can take pride in how she looks and carries herself. When they talked about this, they talked about how women downgrade themselves in how they dress and how they felt it's a cry for attention (*insecurity*), which will get you in the One of Many category (See chart).
2. Beautiful personality—Kind, good sense of humor, considerate, modest.
3. Good conversationalist—Someone who knows themselves, smart, educated.
4. Ambitious—Someone who has a plan for her life. They say this is a major turn-on.

The Turn-offs:

1. Attention-seeking—They say they hate it when a woman is loud. They feel it could mean she always needs attention, either from him or someone else.
2. Bad hygiene—Bad breath, body odor, hair not being clean, unkempt nails (chewed nails, overgrown cuticles), etc.
3. Insecurities—Be confident in yourself and know that you possess beautiful qualities and characteristics.

Choosing to be single doesn't make you a horrible person, it just simply means that you'd rather be alone than with the wrong person!

You should never let anyone pressure you to be with anyone you feel in your heart is not for you, not even yourself!

I did a survey with a few guys, asking various questions. I wanted to do this segment to get a guy's perspective of women. It was one of my favorite parts to do in this book and very interesting! The interviewees come from different races and ages.

Interview with A.C.

B.Y.O.B.: What qualities do you think are needed to keep a relationship healthy and strong?

A.C.: The ability to say whatever to your partner and not be judged or criticized. I want a relationship where I can say to my mate whatever is on my mind and not be judged. I say what's on my mind to start a healthy dialogue. Also mutual respect, being open to participate in one another's worlds freely and willingly.

B.Y.O.B.: How important is it to you for a woman to know who she is?

A.C.: It is critical. As the man in her life, it is my responsibility to show her how important she is and the value that she brings into my life. It is also crucial that I support her in any endeavor. However, I don't feel that it is my place to have to constantly validate her. No matter how beautiful the package, that is so unattractive. Beauty for me in a woman is not just her outward appearance. That confidence, that swagger, is such a turn-on for me. Because that lets me know she believes in herself. That means she can stand. That means she will have the courage to say what is on her mind and not let it fester and cause problems and divide us. A woman knowing who she is will make you want to work to hold her attention, versus the relationship simply becoming complacent or boring.

B.Y.O.B.: If a woman knows herself and has self-confidence and knows what she wants out of life, does that cause insecurities for a man?

A.C.: No, just the opposite—you simply have to step up and be the man. Open doors, be attentive, be supportive, allow her to fall in love with your mental game. Raise the standards above the other guys who did not last. So when temptation arises she will reflect on what we have and what we're working toward. She will have to decide if the risk is worth it.

B.Y.O.B.: What types of characteristics do a woman who knows herself have that can help a man be his best?

A.C.: Strength to stand for what she knows is right, even if I get mad. A woman who has the ability to be soft and encouraging, but yet holds me accountable. A woman who loves the Lord and prays.

B.Y.O.B.: Wow! Okay, thanks. Great response. Thanks, A.C.

A.C.: You're welcome.

Interview with Charles Odom

B.Y.O.B.: As a married man, what are some of the things you would do to help your wife if she had issues with her self-confidence or self-esteem?

Charles: Well, I always tell my wife she is hot, or pretty, or beautiful, or something along those lines every day. But I also take her out to get a new dress sometimes and anything else I need to buy her to keep her feeling great about herself. But I would say the best thing to do is just keep the verbal compliments coming.

B.Y.O.B.: What are some misconceptions that women have about what a man looks for in a woman, along with weight, skin color, etc.?

Charles: I think black women believe that if a man chooses to date or marry a woman outside of his own race, it means that he doesn't like his own race. I think that is crazy. You like who you like. I also think that women underestimate how important a woman's brain is. Honestly, all men are somewhat controlling and demanding to a small degree. Women, in my opinion, prefer strong men who can lead. However, I don't think any man, including me, just wants a woman who will lie down and take anything. We guys need to be checked sometimes, and we want women who are strong and smart in addition to being FYNE.

B.Y.O.B.: In your opinion, does a woman who knows herself, has self-confidence, and knows what she wants out of life cause insecurities for a man?

Charles: No! Do I need to say anything else? Okay, I will. There's nothing more attractive than a woman who is confident in her beauty and brains, but not to the point of arrogance. Women who are insecure make men uncomfortable and are less desirable. I don't want a woman who is trying to be the man in a relationship, but she has to know what and who she is if I am going to go out for the chase.

B.Y.O.B.: What characteristics in a woman can help her man be the best that he can be?

Charles: So let's be sure I understand the question. You want to know what characteristics a woman who knows herself have that can help a man be his best?

B.Y.O.B.: Yes!

Charles: Hmm. I would say she can tell her man the truth no matter what, but if she ever disagrees with him she should only do so in private, never publicly, but she should be confident enough to say in private, "That is not a good idea." But also she has to be able to not always share her opinion, because sometimes a man needs to fail to grow, so even if she doesn't support something, sometimes you have to go with it and let him be him as long as it isn't anything crazy. She also needs to be able to pick up the pieces in case he does fail because no one's opinion matters more than the wife, so she needs to be able to build him back up and continue to believe in him when he fails. One more thing, she listens and gives feedback. Men prefer and are built to lead. And I think women want men to lead, but also we need criticism from life choices and ideas, so she has to listen and communicate.

B.Y.O.B.: Wow! Okay, thanks. (Laughing) One of these really had me saying "Ouch," but I know it's the truth. And that is "But also she has to be able to not always share her opinion because sometimes a man needs to fail to grow, so even if she doesn't support something, sometimes you have to go with it and let him be him as long as it isn't anything crazy." You know that's a hard pill to swallow, right? Especially coming from someone who never wants to see my other half fail, but I know it shouldn't be viewed that way.

Charles: Well, this is a man's perspective so no matter how hard the pill is to swallow, it needs to go down—drink as much water as you like.

B.Y.O.B.: (Laughing) It's the truth. Wow, thanks.

Charles: You're welcome.

Interview with Jimmie Marasigan

B.Y.O.B.: What qualities do you think are needed to keep a relationship healthy and strong?

Jimmie: Being honest and knowing how to compromise.

B.Y.O.B.: What are the pros and cons of a woman who knows herself in relationship to her man?

Jimmie: Pros are the woman knows the right time to joke and when to be serious. Cons are the woman has the power to manipulate the relationship. For instance, if she doesn't get what she wants, she'll give her partner attitude—the "silent treatment," pouting, arguing, or just being downright rude or mean.

B.Y.O.B.: As a married man, what are some of the things you would do to help your wife if she had issues with her self-confidence or self-esteem?

Jimmie: First and foremost, find out what she thinks she lacks, then help her overcome that weakness, fear, or shortcoming.

B.Y.O.B.: Do you think a woman who knows herself and has self-confidence and knows what she wants out of life, does that cause insecurities for a man?

Jimmie: Not for me! I admire and love women that are self-determining—able to think and act accordingly. To me, a woman with self-confidence is a woman that is very independent.

B.Y.O.B.: Wow. I am really shocked by your response since you always play around. (Laughing) Thanks!

Jimmie: I had to really give some thought to it. (Laughing) You're welcome.

Interview with Cardinal

B.Y.O.B.: How important is it for you for a woman to know who she is?

Cardinal: I feel it's very important. Kind of like you said earlier, she can help me love her in a way she would admire and want without a lot of fussing and fighting. I feel that she would have a better sense of security about herself, meaning not having a low self-esteem. Because with her not knowing who she is, it makes it easier for her to get taken advantage of. Then, too, making the man feel insecure about his relationship with her, 'cause of her maybe being gullible or more easily swayed by other men. I'm sure there are other disadvantages to a woman not really knowing her worth and who she is, so it is very important, and one mistake a lot of women make. You can't expect him to know things about you if you can't even figure it out for yourself. Most women should already have a sense of self and how they want to be loved, which started when they were little girls. Life experiences help to mold women and at that point you start to develop *you*. It's really important to set expectations not only of her, but of others as well. Things don't always go as planned, however, because we are all human. If you don't stand up for something, you will fall for anything, as the saying goes. Also, her knowing herself sets a basis for me. That way I will know what she wants and doesn't want and what she will and won't deal with.

B.Y.O.B.: Nice response, thanks.

Cardinal: Welcome.

Interview with Anonymous

B.Y.O.B.: What are some misconceptions that women have about what a man looks for in a woman, along with weight, skin color, etc.?

Anonymous.: While physical attraction is important, a high self-esteem and good attitude is much more important than physical appearance. A physically attractive woman who has low self-esteem is less appealing than a heavier woman who is confident in herself.

B.Y.O.B.: What qualities do you think are needed to keep a relationship healthy and strong?

Anonymous.: I think couples who are dating tend to wait too long to discuss general positions regarding morals, politics, and finances. People want to avoid discussing items that can cause conflicts or reduce a person's appeal. While this makes the initial dating experiences more pleasant and carefree, people may be more invested than intended when they learn of their potential partner's stance on critical issues.

B.Y.O.B.: What characteristics of a woman who knows who she is can help her man be the best that he can be?

Anonymous.: The most important characteristic is for both parties to show interest in their mate on a daily basis. I know of several couples where one party asks about the other person's day and then that individual talks so much about themselves and their day that the other person has lost interest in sharing details.

B.Y.O.B.: Thanks.

Anonymous.: You are welcome!

Interview with a dude they call "Frank"

B.Y.O.B.: There are many characteristics that embody a woman who knows who she is. What characteristics would those be, do you think?

Frank: To me, a woman should embody characteristics that mirror the will of God, meaning things like selflessness, loyalty, respectability, morality, caring, loving, etc., and more often than not a man will be drawn toward those things. But it has to be understood that those qualities should be pleasing to the woman herself and not specifically designated for what a man is looking for. The purpose of your book is looking within yourself, so these characteristics should be practiced in everyday life, and not only pertaining to men. A real man will notice those things before an outer appearance.

B.Y.O.B.: What characteristics of a woman who knows who she is can help her man be the best that he can be?

Frank: Those same qualities should be mirrored in both partners, so it really isn't about specifically conforming to what she brings to her man, but what they bring to each other and those qualities (on both ends) will help both parties.

B.Y.O.B.: How could you, as a man, add to or nourish your woman's self-confidence or knowledge of who she is so that she can continue to grow?

Frank: A man can help a woman's confidence *only* if she is willing to accept his view of her—otherwise it doesn't matter what he says or does. So my answer to the question is that a man can nourish a woman's confidence by giving her mental and emotional support and having her back in all areas of life. Letting her know that her self-image may be lower than what others can plainly see. But it only works when the woman can accept the nourishment and grow from it. You understand what I'm saying? I hope so!

B.Y.O.B.: I really do understand what you are saying. (Laughing) Thank you so much for your honesty in all your responses.

Frank: Welcome!

Rare Beauties (My Single Babies)

Are you single? So am I (for right now). I believe that my "love" will come.

For me, and I know for a lot of you, it's by choice. As I stated earlier, I'd rather be by myself and happy with myself than be with someone that can't and won't love me for who I am! I *refuse*; you and I don't have to settle.

I'm waiting on the right person for me. I always tell people he doesn't have to be perfect, but just the right fit for me.

So, my Rare Beauties, I'm telling you its okay to wait. Wait for the right one God has created simply for you! I'm not going to sit here and write to you and tell you that it's easy—*it's not*. I see a lot of people that seem like they are happy and in love, when really they are all torn up on the inside, confused and looking for freedom within themselves, and they can't find it—not even in the other person. Please, Rare Beauties, take your time and *wait*. The grass is not always greener on the other side. I will say truthfully, God has made this journey worth my while. I have gotten to know who I am, love who I am, and I'm still finding out a lot of things about myself. And I honestly feel if I wait on the right one who has also learnt to love who he has become within himself and in God, we will be one heck of a team: the threefold of God, my husband, and me.

I also know that we will have our ups and downs, but that's okay. Every relationship does. The difference will be we have God, our friendship, and our foundation (we know how to communicate).

I'm ready. Are you . . . my Rare Beauties?

Devin Brown

Rare Beauties Guidelines/Letter

- Spend time with people who like you and care about you.
- Ignore (and stay away from) people who put you down or treat you badly.
- Do things that you enjoy or that make you feel good.
- Do things you are good at.
- Reward yourself for your successes.
- Develop your talents.
- Be your own best friend—treat yourself well and do things that are good for you.
- Make good choices for yourself, and don't let others make your choices for you.
- Take responsibility for yourself, your choices, and your actions.
- Always do what you believe is right.
- Be true to yourself and your values.
- Respect other people and treat them right.
- Set goals and work to achieve them.

Health

I spoke earlier about how my weight went from one hundred and forty pounds to about two hundred pounds and this was throughout high school. As I got older, I got up to nearly three hundred pounds. I was so unhappy. So as I began to work on the inside, the great changes that were happening to my inner self were not reflected on the outside. On the inside, I had lifted a lot of heavy burdens with God's help and I became lighter, so it was like I was carrying a too-big outer shell. I can remember my grandmother would tell me how beautiful I was; it was so funny as I remember times when she would say, "Little gal, you starting to pick up a little weight." I would drop whatever I was doing to do some sit-ups. She said it with so much love and compassion, and I had missed it! It was like she would keep me grounded, and I loved her for that. My grandmother suffered from high blood pressure. It runs in the family; my mom and my middle sister are now battling high blood pressure. I am so grateful that even at almost three hundred pounds I didn't have high blood pressure or diabetes; the only thing that I dealt with was severe back pain. I began to walk, and even though my eating habits didn't change completely, I would make small adjustments, yet still I hardly lost any weight. My metabolism was very low from all these years of being a "couch potato."

I'm not saying this to sway anyone to do this, but what happened to work for me was to get a gastric bypass. This is a weight-loss surgery, and it was a hard decision for me. With the help and support of family and friends and lots of research and consultation with my doctor, I finally made the decision to go through with it. I have now lost over seventy pounds, and I am feeling wonderful. I really have made a life-changing decision; I try to exercise at least three times a day. I try to remember when I have something heavy on my mind to not drown it out with food.

Devin Brown

My Rare Beauties, what I'm trying to say for those of you that are in school—middle school, high school, college, trade school, whatever—stay active and please exercise. Do things that keep your heart racing. Love yourself enough to do that. Even if you have gained a lot of weight like I did, get with positive people or make your own little group where you guys go walking or play some kind of sport. I have seen a lot of people do it without surgery.

Someone that inspired me so much goes to my church; her name is Cathy Burford. A very beautiful lady, she was also heavy and was not happy with her appearance. Then she began to eat healthy and exercise a lot. She began to lose weight and now she is very happy with herself, and she looks good, if I might add. She is a very positive person, she inspires me in that area of my life, and I try to now exercise more and eat right. So if you are reading this, thank you, Cathy—thank you so much, you add to this area of my life.

I also got braces to make some changes to my teeth, to have a more beautiful smile. These are all the things that I did to make my outer appearance match my inside manifestation. I love myself right now.

It's important that we, as women, get ourselves taken care of: our yearly exams, most of all staying worry-free, and continue to love ourselves the proper way.

Remember, its mind over body. If you change your mind-set, your body will follow.

Goals

Let me tell you a story. This was inspired by a true story, but I put my own twist to it.

There were three young ladies who became best friends. What's crazy is they had their birthdays on the same day. They were talking about their plans for their birthdays. One was having a big birthday bash—an all-out party. The second one was getting an outfit with shoes, and the third said her parents were investing in stocks for her.

The girl whose parents invested in the stocks was learning about investment and how to make her money grow. Her parents were teaching her things that were going to help her throughout life and not just giving her things that provided temporary gratification.

I grew up believing as long as I had a good job with good benefits, I was doing well and to keep it. That is true if you don't have your own dreams. I have always dreamed of being a nurse, a teacher, a photographer, and so on and so on. I never became any of that. I got a good job and stayed there. I never truly believed I could be what I wanted to be—it was too impossible, or so I thought. I was so wrong.

I was reunited with one of my friends from years ago, and he came to me and he had all these big dreams in mind. I thought, "Boy, you are really crazy. You are not going to be able to do this and that." But what really happened is that he planted a seed in me and gave me something to really think about. I also had another friend, my manager. She watered that seed, and I began to dream again, but this time I began to put my actions toward my dreams. And I saw them coming to life. I realized that even though I have a good job with good insurance, I was working on someone else's dream and not my own.

Devin Brown

So, my Rare Beauties, if you are in school, go and keep going to get your education. Know what it is that you want out of life and make it happen—don't give up. I just recently reunited with my one of my teachers, and she told me that her oldest daughter is sixteen years old, and by the time she graduates from high school, she will be graduating with an associate's degree. How awesome is that? This encouraged me a lot. If she can do it, you can do it. I was speechless to hear this; it made my heart smile to see young ladies doing so well in these times.

I want to leave this chapter by saying: you never know who you will inspire or how many lives you might change by simply being you. Love yourself, know yourself, and live out your dreams. Make sure you dress up to where you'd like to be and not where you are in life.

I hope that I have either planted a seed in someone or watered what's already there. Either way, start putting action toward your dreams, because we all know that faith without work is dead and useless.

B.Y.O.B.
(Be Your Own Beautiful)

I am my own beautiful; God created me to be humbly unique and rare.

I am my own beautiful; I inspire others by simply being me.

I am my own beautiful because I have found myself . . . How do I know? Well, because I have stopped seeking validations from others.

I am my own beautiful because I have found happiness within myself.

I am my own beautiful; I know that I don't have to have an hourglass-shaped figure, but that a healthy way of life is very important.

I am my own beautiful; every day I promise myself that I will walk boldly and upright in front of God, myself, and others. I will surround myself with positive people; I will also make positive steps every day toward my goals and dreams. I will succeed, for I know that coming out of my comfort zone will bring me closer to my destiny.

Why?

Because *I am my own beautiful!*

Devin Brown

Me at a Cherise's birthday party! my Hair was done by Rikki Burke

The day of my photo shoot for my book cover, Mrs. Destiny McGill
doing my make-up . . . "whipping my beauty into shape."

Devin Brown

My trip to Denver, Colorado

My baby sister Aundrea and my niece Amari
(Amari loves taking pictures . . . LOL she's always ready!)

Devin Brown

My middle sister Raetequa "Sharae"

My nephew Kendale and Niece Keidyn

Devin Brown

My Mother—Karen

My grandmother "granny" Mary D. Jackson

Devin Brown

B.Y.O.B. Interviews

In the second part of my book I wanted to concentrate on outer beauty. In the first part, I touch on how important it was to me to have my outer appearance match my inner beauty! So what I have done is gather those I thought had a God-given talent to discuss topics they were gifted in and did interview setups to give us advice on how we can apply these things to help us create who we are and have it actually reflected in our outer appearance. I was so moved by these interviews and learned so much from them. I have actually begun to apply much of the advice to my own lifestyle.

INTERVIEW WITH:

Destiny McGill

"Whipping your Beauty into Shape" ~ Destiny

MAKEUP

"And the LORD answered me, and said, Write the vision, and
make [it] plain upon tables, that he may run that readeth it . . ."
~ Habbakuk 2:2 ~
Destiny's Forte: "Where Beauty Begins and Music Never Ends"

Professional Vocalist / Pro Makeup Artist / Certified Eyelash Extension Technician

Destiny Deshea McGill, (July 27, 1981), is known simply as Destiny. She has been the noble wife of nine years to Eric McGill, honored mother of two with one on the way, and the proud owner of *Whip Lash* Salon & Boutique. Destiny also has aspirations to become a nationally known contemporary-gospel artist. She was born and raised in Dallas, Texas, where she attended Booker T. Washington High School for the Performing and Visual Arts Magnet. There she studied classical music with an emphasis in Opera. Growing up, she was exposed to an array of genres. Her first foray into singing came in church at the age of thirteen. Later she began to sing with choirs and groups and played acting roles in theater.

She began to showcase her talent in various venues throughout the Dallas-Fort Worth area. As her confidence increased and style developed, Destiny auditioned for Fred Hammond and currently sings soprano as a background vocalist, continuously traveling around the world to places such as Canada, Barbados, London, Nigeria, Trinidad, and more. Thankfully her humbleness has not been compromised. She is featured singing background vocals on Tamela Mann's single, Kirk Franklin's promotional single, and Fred Hammond's latest CD *God, Love, and Romance* along with the previous album *Love Unstoppable*, available in stores now.

Devin Brown

After realizing that her passion of performing included understanding makeup application for stage, Destiny began researching to do some hands-on training. Through it all, an entirely newfound desire began to rise up within her! Now she enjoys the artistry of beauty and is fascinated with the level of confidence seen in every client moments before their makeup is complete. Makeup is no longer just a hobby, but now has evolved into her ministry for increasing the self-esteem of young girls and mature women as she teaches them how to *"Be Your OWN Beautiful!"* From that point on, Destiny dedicated herself to following up with new trends. For example, she became a certified eyelash extension technician as a means of offering another service to her divas. The looks that Destiny provides are complementary to the everyday woman that stems from young ladies preparing for prom, to homemakers, to even walking the red carpet!

While pursuing her career as a soloist, makeup artist, and eyelash extension technician, each ambition of hers continues to grow with the help of the Almighty. She keeps God first and only goes where He tells her to go. Destiny is destined for greatness.

B.Y.O.B.: I first want to say thank you for inviting me to your studio; it's beautiful inside here. I see that you are doing some great things with the space. I'm ready to come get my makeup done.

Destiny: Absolutely. (Laughing)

B.Y.O.B.: I was saying earlier that I enjoyed the partnership of you and your husband. I think that is so beautiful. I love stuff like that. (Laughing) But God really works because you are one with your husband.

Destiny: Absolutely.

B.Y.O.B.: Before we start, I know you just got off the road with Fred Hammond.

Destiny: Yes, I did!

B.Y.O.B.:   How was that?

Destiny: It was tiring because we had night after night of shows. And because we were headliners, we had to perform last so that means we come off the stage the latest, which means we get to our hotel the latest. We will get to our hotel about one o'clock in the morning and have to be back up at three thirty or four to catch a six fifteen or six forty-five flight. Once we land, it's about ten in the morning and we immediately have to go to the venue for sound check. Once the sound check is completely done, then we go back to the hotel. We have only about three hours to take a nap, but you didn't really get to sleep the night before, so it was a constant of turnaround and shows and flying. We actually did six flights in three days.

B.Y.O.B.:   That's a lot.

Destiny: Yes, it is a lot!

B.Y.O.B.:   So you guys were on the road for six days?

Destiny: No. Three days and six flights.

B.Y.O.B.:   Wow!

Destiny: It is; it is! (Laughing)

B.Y.O.B.:   So you have been singing with Fred Hammond for a while, right?

Destiny: Four and a half years.

B.Y.O.B.:   Wow. That is a long time and a blessing.

Destiny: It is! I have been on two of his most recent CDs, and I have cut some things (records) for Tamela Mann and Kirk Franklin recently.

Devin Brown

B.Y.O.B.:   Really?

Destiny: I have been working with him diligently.

B.Y.O.B.:   So are you looking into pursuing a singing career?

Destiny: I'm not sure, Devin.

(We both laugh.)

Destiny: I'm not sure; you know how people encourage you and say you should do this, and you should do that? At the end of the day when I lay my head on my pillow, I think "Lord, whatever your will is for me, for my life."

B.Y.O.B.:   Absolutely.

Destiny: Sometimes we do get lost in what other people see for us, but really the only thing they see is what they expect for you, and even though they have that wish doesn't mean that's what God has prepared for your life. If He (God) doesn't ever allow me to do a project of my own, He has already done magnificent things; I have been in and out of the country, not on my dime, at least ten or fifteen times.

B.Y.O.B.:   Really?

Destiny: Yes! God is good!

B.Y.O.B.:   Wow.

Destiny: I just thank Him (God). He is so good. I just came back from a free cruise (laughing). We performed those first two nights and then we had like three more nights on that cruise free, just free days to do what we wanted to do—relax, chill, whatever. I just said thank you, Lord, and took pictures of the water. You just look at God's magnificent work; he created that beauty for us!

Devin Brown

B.Y.O.B.: Right! And not everybody can experience that.

Destiny: Absolutely! I'm almost across the world . . . I'm in Cuba! It's not what you see at home; it's like life exists outside Dallas. (We both laugh.) Oak Cliff, Pleasant Grove . . .

B.Y.O.B.: (Laughing) Right!

Destiny: Galveston is not the only place that has a beach. (Laughing.) You actually can go somewhere else! But it was nice.

B.Y.O.B.: So you spent Mother's Day on the road?

Destiny: Yes! On the road.

B.Y.O.B.: WOW! That is so awesome, Destiny!

Destiny: Thank you! Thank You!

B.Y.O.B.: Do you feel that looking and feeling beautiful is important to a woman's confidence and self-esteem? And if so, why?

Destiny: I think it is important as far as self-esteem because when you are doing your makeup in the mirror, you are basically enhancing what you find to be just off the chain. Like, Father, when you created this part of my face, you did that! (We both laugh.) So you can kind of tell when you look at a woman and she has a lot of blush on, you can tell she really likes emphasizing her cheekbones. When you see a lady who wears red lipstick and purple or with these vibrant colors, she loves her lips. And if you see a lady really emphasize her brows or the lid of her eyes or things of that nature, she really likes the way her eyes look! So I do believe that it plays a part, because when you are doing your makeup you are looking at yourself while you are doing it and when you are complete and you walk out the door, you think *I did this much to my face and now I'm going to go out into the world. I'm confident, and I'm ready, and I know I look good.* Therefore,

Devin Brown

when you go out, that confidence is not only going to show on the outside, it's going to be pumping on the inside.

B.Y.O.B.: Right.

Destiny: Yes! So it's like when you first start applying the makeup you are not really there, but as soon as the face is done . . . You start whipping that hair to the back and you are gone!

B.Y.O.B.: (Laughing) I know I feel that way. When I put a little makeup on I think "oh my gosh!"

Destiny: Yes, when I finish a client's makeup I need her to act like when she first walked through the door. Because I don't think her head is going to fit out the door. (We laugh.)

B.Y.O.B.: You're probably going to be telling me that.

Destiny: You know what? It's beautiful. I like that you can see the confidence immediately elevate . . . It's wonderful!

B.Y.O.B.: What is the most important beauty advice that you can give to women?

Destiny: Beauty advice that I can give to a woman is to drink lots of water on a daily basis. Hydrating your skin is one of the most important things you can do before makeup application. The smoothness of your skin when it's moisturized is great, and you need to maintain moisture—healthy moisture, not the sweat. That would be the most important; you need healthy skin before applying all these other elements to your skin. No matter how natural people say it is, or organic, there are still chemicals within the makeup. We should do our part by making sure that our skin is always healthy, that way when the makeup has been washed off, we still look good.

B.Y.O.B.: Exactly! I like that! You know when you think about drinking water you think about drinking it to lose weight, but you never think about what affect it has on your skin. So I like that!

B.Y.O.B.:   What are some common beauty mistakes that women make, that you notice?

Destiny: I have noticed the heavy lip liner. The distinguishing look of how you put your lip liner on and your lipstick—it's like the line is so dark. It's either the black or the brown, and then you go in with the silver and the red but the line is still not blending in. What I would say with the lining of the lips is to take a lip brush or your finger and blend it down and work it around, but still keep the smooth edge and then apply your lip gloss or your lipstick instead of leaving the line.

Another thing I have noticed is some women go heavy-handed with their eyebrows. I will advise you that it's not cute to wear a heavy brow; it is not supposed to look painted on or look like a clown; it's supposed to look natural. Shaving your eyebrows and then painting on a fake brow looks odd—it's far better to strategically pluck your brows and then lightly use an eyebrow pencil if necessary.

B.Y.O.B.:   What do you think about the red lipstick coming back?

Destiny: I think that it's awesome! I love the red lipstick. I don't think red lipstick and purple eye shadow, orange shadow, or even black and all that, but if you are going to do such a vibrant red lip then your eye should be nude and as natural as possible. Choose one feature to play up: do I want to emphasize my lips more or my eyes? Not both—choose one. Both will work well if you're doing a photo shoot or if you are going for a dramatic look. But for a night on the town or you just want to look extra sexy, then yes, you can do the red lipstick but keep the eyes natural. (Laughing.) You could even do the "cat eyes" with your liner, but as far as your shadow I would say keep it as natural as possible.

Devin Brown

B.Y.O.B.: I remember back in the day when I was younger I would wear red lipstick, and people after a while would tell me that it was no-no, but I see it coming back again.

Destiny: Absolutely! It's coming back in style. You know how things are—they come and go!

B.Y.O.B.: Exactly!

B.Y.O.B.: How would you describe your signature look and what is it about your style that sets you apart from other makeup artists?

Destiny: My signature look is more casual. I'm not a flamboyant type of person. If people catch me in the streets I may or may not have on makeup. (Laughing.) I'm a mom, wife, and entrepreneur, so I'm on the go a lot of the time. If I'm going to pick my son up, or I have a day off, or I'm going to have lunch with friends, and I don't have to put on a full face of makeup, I'm game. You are probably going to see me without it—you would probably see me with lip gloss on and I'm straight! Now if I'm going out and I do have to put a little makeup on . . . my face is very exotic-looking, so if I overdo it I'm going to look like a drag queen. (Laughing.) You need to know your lane, what lane are you in (laughing), so basically I like to be as casual and fresh as possible, so that is my signature look.

B.Y.O.B.: Because in all honestly I didn't know you did makeup.

Destiny: Yeah. (Laughing.) A lot of people say "Destiny, if you do makeup then you need to have it on," and I think "What? I don't know! Do I?" (Laughing.) I don't know about putting on makeup every day. I did say I was going to try to get a little bit better and try to apply something every now and then, but that's another issue with me because I'm a very humble person.

Devin Brown

B.Y.O.B.:   Right! I know!

Destiny: So I don't always broadcast what I'm doing or the new adventure that God is captivating me on. I really just like to walk in it and see where He is taking me first, because sometimes when we make a left and there's a candy shop, it doesn't mean He wants you to stop, he just wants you to walk past it. But if you tell everybody "Oh, I'm about to go to this candy shop to the left," they'll all reply "Oh, you're about to get some candy? Well, don't forget to get me some." But then I did go by there, but I didn't actually go in, so I don't like to throw things out there. Yeah, so it's when people ask you to do makeup to the level where you do First Lady Jakes and Yolanda Adams, you have to be really good . . . I don't know.

B.Y.O.B.:   (Laughing) I know, because I'm sitting here speechless. I knew you sang but I didn't know you did makeup.

Destiny: Yes! I have done some things with BET. I did the makeup for *Sunday Best's* Erica and Tina Campbell, Donnie McClurkin, Kirk Franklin, that whole lineup. I did their makeup for the show when they were here in Dallas last year.

B.Y.O.B.:   So let me ask you how you even get booked for makeup when people really don't know that you do it.

Destiny: That's the thing; that's how I know it's my Father in Heaven. Well in the case of First Lady Jakes (Bishop T.D. Jakes's wife), I was called by one of her assistants. She said she was referred to me to do makeup, and I agreed. (Laughing.) It was out of the blue, but I just went with it. I didn't want to ask who referred me, because that's not important. Obviously it was someone who knew me because she had my number. Well, come to find out, it was this weaveologist I model for here in Dallas. She does hair and a lot of weave, and she wanted to use me as a model for the class. I did, and her makeup artist didn't show up for some reason. I didn't have any of my brushes or tools, but they asked if I could just make it work. So I was using my fingers and paper towels and trying to get it together because we had a photographer there to do a photo shoot. So long story short, I did the makeup and she said, "Oh my God, if you can do amazing work with your hands, just imagine what you could do if you had actual makeup brushes!" It is so ironic that the makeup artist didn't show up; it's funny how God works. He just does that. That class was last October, and I got the call this past March with First Lady Jakes.

B.Y.O.B.: That's so cool.

Destiny: So as time has passed, my mind isn't saying "oh, I did this makeup with my fingers; I know I'm about to get a job." No! (Sighing.) So she does so many celebrities' hair that she flies in and out of Dallas, back and forth in LA. They fly to her, so she is really referring me a lot. So I may be doing the makeup for the opening of *Sparkle* when they do the red carpet.

B.Y.O.B.: Really!

Destiny: Yeah, so I'm just excited!

B.Y.O.B.: Destiny, I'm excited for you!

Destiny: I just thank God because I don't . . . (Eyes tearing up, she clears her throat.)

B.Y.O.B.: Okay if you start to cry, I will too!

(We both share a laugh.)

Destiny: It is so amazing in what He does, and when you are faithful to Him, and you live for Him, you don't have to worry about who sees you living for Him or prove anything to anybody, because He sees you! He says, "I see you, I have you, and I know what I'm going to do for you, and I have it under control." It's an amazing blessing. Oh my God, it's like when you wake up in the morning and you don't take it for granted! Like when they were calling me for BET, I was just in shock when he said, "Yes, this is an executive from BET." I said, "Oh Lord, (laughing), let me take a breath." Same thing happened with Kirk Franklin. We were on the cruise and someone saw me singing with Fred Hammond, and a week later when I came back from the cruise they told Kirk to call me and he did . . . to come sing! He said he had a show that night and would I be able to make it? Of course I did, and the next thing I knew, Kirk was pulling up for his session . . . and I have been on call every week.

B.Y.O.B.: WOW! So this is not just here in Dallas?

Destiny: No, they are here in Dallas.

B.Y.O.B.: Oh, okay.

Destiny: It's like, Father, I don't know what you are doing, but it's those types of things and those magnitudes of blessing. Not that I take anything smaller that He does for me for granted, because I don't, but I don't understand . . . I don't even want to understand it because I might pass out.

B.Y.O.B.: Oh, you will pass out (laughing) because you can't comprehend the work of God.

Destiny: (Laughing.) Devin, I might pass out. I said "God, in the name of Jesus, what art thou doing with my life?" (Laughing.)

B.Y.O.B.: But you know what? You are inspiring me so much right now! Because even with my book—it's small to me and I just want to touch one person. I would like for it to go global and go all over the country, but if it can just touch one person and cause them to change, I'm okay. I have had people come up to me since I have been writing this book and say, "Oh, you are going to be on *The Talk*." I'm receiving it, but my mind is saying, "I don't see it."

People tell me all the time you don't know where your book is going to go, but I promise you it's going make it big! All I know is God put it on my heart to do, and I'm just being obedient and doing it!

Destiny: That's all He asks us to do! And at the end of the day he just wants us to live according His Word and be good children and be obedient. You might have to sacrifice some things or lose some things, but know that He is always with you. He said he'd never leave you nor forsake you. Yes, you are in a storm but I'm still here.

B.Y.O.B.: I was just telling someone that God is so faithful, even when we are not. I have been saying that all year long. Destiny you just don't know—you have been a testimony.

Destiny: Amen. You know that is just a piece because I'm telling you; have you ever seen that *Beetlejuice* movie when that guy's head shrank down real little? That's how I am feeling. (Laughing.)

I think "God, when you're done, do it again—I don't know what to do!" (Laughing.) This is a ride we are on. We are driving and rolling and we are in and out of places, and yet if we didn't have that seatbelt of grace and that buckle of mercy, we wouldn't even be here.

B.Y.O.B.: You are so right; I know I wouldn't be here. I know it's mind-blowing.

Destiny: It is! And just recently I did the ex-wife of Nate Newton (the hall of famer) of the Dallas Cowboys. I didn't know who she was and she wrote a book called *Silent Tears* and her book is growing—she's all over the world. Like I said, I didn't know who she was, but I was like Whoa! You never know who God puts in your path for any reason and she was saying to me she was grateful that God but me in her path as her makeup artist.

B.Y.O.B.: Wow.

Destiny: Things have been turning around and I just say "Father . . ." That's why I just want to walk with Him. People pull and say I want you over here or come over there because we are doing this with so and so. I'm not judging anybody, because I'm not saying if you don't love God that I can't be around you, but at the end of the day I have to try the spirit by the spirit. And if your spirit is not willing and you're doing all these other things then instead of me judging you, I need to separate, because when people disconnect themselves from you and you disconnect yourself from them, obviously they weren't attached to your destiny, and I'm not just saying that because that's my name. (We share a laugh.) But I'm just saying they were not attached to your destiny so leave them alone.

B.Y.O.B.: Absolutely . . . I would have never imagined that our paths would cross again.

Destiny: I know!

B.Y.O.B.: I would have never guessed, but one thing is when I began to write this book I prayed and asked God to move. So I didn't go around wondering who I was going to get to do this and that—I felt God move and say this is who I want you to get to do this part and that part (for the interviews). I was like, okay, God, and I had peace behind it; I just let God lead me. So yes, I never thought that our paths would cross again. But I'm glad!

Destiny: Me too! Because I never thought it either; especially in this way—me doing makeup and it's not like I never had the passion but the only reason why I started wearing makeup was because I was on the road and going on stage. I was twenty-six and trying to learn how to put on makeup. My family didn't wear it, so I was never taught how to wear it, and I got into it that way. I started having children, so I was thinking, "Oh Lord, I got to do something and have my own schedule and be able to help my husband." I don't believe in just leaving it all on him—we are a team. There is no way if the lights get cut off I will be looking at him like "What are you going to do," or "Oh, you should have been . . ." No, that's not right. (We share a laugh.) Yes, he can carry most of the load, but I can help!

B.Y.O.B.: Yes, totally! (Laughing.)

Destiny: So that's what I was doing! I was selling Mary Kay and then I went to selling Mocha and I went to Glam RX, and now I'm solo.

B.Y.O.B.: So did you actually go to school for it?

Destiny: No, I didn't! That's why I'm amazed. I just really started doing makeup last year.

B.Y.O.B.: Wow! So who does your makeup while you are on the road?

Destiny: Me! And others ask me to do their makeup . . . It would be at one point in time they would say, "Oh, uh-uh, you're not touching this face!" (We laugh.) And then when they see my face they'd say "Oh, you did that? Now you can do my face." They weren't ready for me, Devin! (Laughing) But they're ready for me now.

B.Y.O.B.: That is too funny! So now I have to ask what are some of your favorite products in your makeup kit?

Destiny: Some of my favorite products would be brow gel . . . I love brow gel.

Devin Brown

B.Y.O.B.:   Okay, tell me what that is.

Destiny: Brow gel is clear and it also comes in colors like copper, auburn, like a red-brown, and just brown. But what it does is it keeps the hairs together. So if you want brown or dark brown, it keeps you from taking that pencil and going too far with it.

B.Y.O.B.:   Ooooh.

Destiny: So once you start with you brow brush, you take it and brush it in because it already has the color on it. If you do it with clear, then you take some brow powder with your brow brush and you just stroke it in, the way your hair grows. Instead of overdoing it with the pencil, especially if you have your face already done and you have taken that pencil too far or you go too heavy and you can't brush it off, because if you do then you have smeared it all over your foundation.

I also love concealer. It covers blemishes, and if you have bags and you can use it under your brow bone, and what that will do is highlight it, making it look sleek and defined. Also if you weren't able to make it to get your eyebrows waxed or threaded then the concealer would cover up those hairs. I love that! So I think those are two of the things that I love most in my kit.

B.Y.O.B.:   What products do you think a woman should have in her purse?

Destiny: Mascara, lip gloss, and a translucent powder.

B.Y.O.B.:   Okay, explain that?

Destiny: A translucent powder is not a color powder—it is more of a powder you can use to take the shine off your face, so many people take their makeup and retouch all they're doing is packing on makeup and clogging up their pores. So I would just keep those things, and maybe a small compact of eye shadow. Maybe if you are coming from work and going to a musical or something and want to throw on some makeup that you wouldn't wear into the office, you will have it. I also want to add that I use all kinds of brands: Mac, Glam RX, Revlon, Maybelline, they all have really good shadows.

B.Y.O.B.: Really! Because as you can see, I have really dark pigment around my eyes . . .

Destiny: Because of your allergies.

B.Y.O.B.: Yes!

Destiny: That is where the drainage is held.

B.Y.O.B.: So I have been doing really well with my makeup, but if I put on a yellow shadow it doesn't show on my eyes.

Destiny: Yes, this normal, especially for the more vibrant colors. If you apply a color that you want to have impact, then you can use primer. They have primer for your eyes, your face, and your lips, and what it does is it's basically a foundation that you put on to hold that color and allow the color to show up. If that doesn't work, then you can use a really light, pale white concealer . . . you would just apply it before the color on that lower lid.

B.Y.O.B.: I don't know if you are familiar with her, but Latasha Wright works out of Atlanta for Rob Ector and she does a lot of work with celebrity makeup. So I just look at her work and try to imitate that, and that is how I've been learning. I do try to make it my own, though.

B.Y.O.B.: Do you believe that sometimes less is more?

Destiny: Yes, I do! Absolutely. You don't want to go to work all heavy. There is a time and place for everything.

Devin Brown

B.Y.O.B.: I personally don't like heavy makeup. I wear Bare Minerals foundation because it's so light and I can't feel it. And it matches my skin tone well!

Destiny: Right! If it doesn't feel airy and your skin feels like it's in a coffin (we both share a laugh), your face can't breathe.

B.Y.O.B.: My book is designed for women in general, but I am targeting young ladies especially. What tips can you give a young woman who is starting to prepare for a special event like prom?

Destiny: Okay, that's easy. I had this one client and she is seventeen and her mom didn't want her to have all this makeup. At the same time, the young lady felt that on her prom night she should get it all. My personal opinion is you want to stay glamorous but yet right for your age, so for those particular clients in that age group I wouldn't dare do the red lipstick because that is more of a sexy look for mature women. I would keep it real soft with pink, mauve, purple, things of that nature, because you want to maintain your youth as much as possible. I understand that you want to be grown, that you feel like "Hey, I want to be grown. I am grown," but when you get those pictures back you're going to be disappointed. People are going to think you look like you're at least twenty-five, and not in a good way. So, yes, I would recommend all young girls use soft shades and not those hard-core colors.

B.Y.O.B.: Even with me being grown, I like soft colors—it stands out to me.

Destiny: Exactly! I don't want to go out looking like a clown.

(We share a laugh.)

B.Y.O.B.: What is the most memorable moment you've had doing someone's makeup?

Devin Brown

Destiny: I would say the most memorable moment would be when I did Kirk Franklin. He was different. He was my first client and it was five in the morning and I was waiting on him and I was all set up and he came in and said, "Oh, that's okay. I don't need any makeup; my wife already did it." I just gave him this blank stare and said, "But I want to do your makeup." (We laughed.) So he left and he came back about thirty minutes later and he said, "My sister, do you have some powder for me?" and I told him, "Sure, have a seat." So he sat down and I knew since he's a man he won't get all the things done a woman does, of course. The fact that he was kind of reluctant but when he opened up and gave me a chance, he was happy—that was great.

B.Y.O.B.: So how do you do a man's makeup? What's the difference between doing a man's makeup and a woman's?

Destiny: See, I still have to use primer for foundation, and I still have to use concealer because they are on TV, so I have to cover up any blemishes, or if they have large pores—things of that nature. I have to go in with this little sponge and wet a little bit if they have a black goatee, for instance, and make it neater . . . So with Kirk, he was very pleased and I would say that would have to be my most memorable moment, just because I never had a person not want their makeup done. They usually come in and have a seat and are ready to go. With him I had everything laid out and it was so pretty and so nice and neat. And I knew he was going to be my first client, so I wanted to make sure I gave a really good first impression. It's like he came in and looked at me and then looked at my station and said no. My feelings were so crushed because I wanted to do his makeup.

There is another memorable moment. I know I do a lot of different people, but when I was with First Lady Jakes, she was so sweet and humble; she is a really nice woman. I was not expecting her to embrace me with a hug and tell me thank you. She was so sincere with her approach, I don't know if I was ready for it. Yes, I know she is in the public light and the Christian scene, but I still expected those at a certain caliber to not really trust any outsiders, so I wasn't really expecting her to talk to me. I have done celebrities where they come in and sit down and don't say a word, or they're on their phone, but she was very nice and asked me how I was. And then when I was done, she was bouncing and saying how cute she looked.

B.Y.O.B.: So does that make you feel good?

Destiny: It makes me feel wonderful. I feel so good inside because she loved it! She never let any makeup artist put fake eyelashes on her, but she let me do it. I knew one of the artists that used to work for her and she told me, "No, she won't let you put eyelashes on her, so don't try because she will tell you no." She didn't tell me no, she just thought she looked cute. First Lady Jakes always asks about me because she is always concerned about my well-being. It's those types of moments that make you not look at someone's status but at where they are in life and see that they are human. That was refreshing because I have run into those that don't care about anyone, they just want people to do what they want and then get out of the way. Don't talk to them, don't smile, don't ask any questions—that kind of attitude.

B.Y.O.B.: Well, it's like you said earlier—they have that guard up.

Destiny: They have a guard up and they have been broken by people they have let in.

B.Y.O.B.: What if you can't afford a dermatologist—what is some advice you can give? Especially for teenagers going through puberty?

Destiny: I would suggest St. Ives. They have this cleanser; it's apricot scrub, and the main ingredient is salicylic acid. It works great for blackheads and those who are acne prone; it's a good scrub and good exfoliate. If you can't find it, the brand Equate works just as well.

B.Y.O.B.: Really?

Destiny: Yes! It's not expensive at all. I have used it and have recommended it to a lot of people and it has worked.

B.Y.O.B.: My face has been breaking out really bad here lately, to the point where I had to give makeup a rest; I don't know why, but I have been assuming that it's because of allergies.

Destiny: I think you should try that Apricot Scrub, even if you have to buy it in the Equate brand. Everyone I have recommended it to has loved it because it not only exfoliates, it breaks down the dead skin where you have dark discoloration. It won't be overnight, but over time you will see a difference.

B.Y.O.B.: What are your techniques for cleaning your makeup brushes?

Destiny: You can go to MAC and get their makeup-brush cleaner. I personally clean my personal brushes at least once every other week. Now, this is for my personal brushes because no one ever uses them but me. I think you should do a deep cleaning once every other month. When I say a deep cleaning, I mean where you take your brushes and submerge them in water and use a mild soap like Johnson's Baby Shampoo and get in there with your fingers.

B.Y.O.B.: And this will not hurt the brush bristles?

Destiny: No, because you are using a mild soap. Now, if you use a strong soap, then yes, it can strip your brushes. You want to submerge your brush first, but you don't want to stand them with the bristles up, because the water will drain down into the brush where the handle is and where the glue holds it together, which could weaken it.

Devin Brown

B.Y.O.B.: So you don't put the whole brush in the water?

Destiny: No, but the brush itself, you can sit them on the side (counter corner) of your sink with a rubber band tied around them and just work your brushes with the mild soap and then lay them flat on a towel, don't stand them up! And make sure all the soap is out.

B.Y.O.B.: (Laughing.) I'm glad you told me that because I would have put the whole brush in the water.

Destiny: So, say for instance you have one shadow brush and you dip it in a cream-color shadow and then you want to use brown, so you want to clean it real quick . . . Sally's has a cleaner, too, and it's not as expensive as MAC. CVS also has a really good brush cleaner, but with theirs you have to rinse off. The ones that I'm talking about, you just spray them on and they dry within seconds and it disinfects and moisturizes your brushes.

B.Y.O.B.: (Laughing) Wow! I am learning! I will be at Sally's like it's a candy store.

B.Y.O.B.: How long should you wait to throw away makeup? When do you know it's old?

Destiny: They have expiration dates on makeup, believe it or not. It seems as though the expiration dates are decreasing for some reason. I don't know if it's the chemicals that they are using now, because at one point things were able to last longer and now they are not. So if I had a foundation and you have those sponges that you continue to use over your face—if you are sweaty or oily, sometimes that sweat or oil is in that puff, and you put it back in your compact and close it and bacteria is growing. That's why I like to use brushes or the throwaway sponges. As far as cream foundation, I will keep them about six months—cream foundation, cream concealer, any of those creams. For powder, I will say about the same;

if you don't use it that much, don't get such a large compact, get something smaller so you aren't throwing your money away.

B.Y.O.B.: Do you feel like you have achieved all your goals as a successful makeup artist?

Destiny: No, I don't.

B.Y.O.B.: What is it you're reaching for?

Destiny: This is going to be big, Devin!

B.Y.O.B.: Okay, come on. I'm ready, because I will stand right behind you!

Destiny: (Laughing.) I want to be at the Academy Awards and hear the best makeup done in a feature film . . . Destiny McGill!

B.Y.O.B.: I love it! I can see that, too, Destiny.

Destiny: (Taking a deep breath) Oh God, did I just say that?

B.Y.O.B.: No, Destiny. That's good, and I can see that.

Destiny: And that is *if* it's God's desire. It's *my* desire and I know You said You will give us the desires of our heart, but You didn't say You will give us all of them. So I say, "Lord, if it's in your will . . ."

B.Y.O.B.: I can see that, and I went with you on that.

(We share a laugh.)

B.Y.O.B.: What does *Be Your Own Beautiful* mean to you?

Destiny: Be Your Own Beautiful means to me, wow, so many things that I struggle with. It's not easy to love yourself when you've heard or believe things about yourself that you have started to think are not true because our Father in Heaven said so. But because of the flesh and we were born into iniquity, we tend to latch on to those negative things. Like I have dealt with some major, major insecurities even in my adult life. With my looks some people would say what are you? Or where are you from? You've got to be something else—you're black and mixed with something and I don't know. But at the end of the day I think "Lord, how I can be beautiful and know that I am beautiful?" It can be hard to do that. It can be really, really hard when you are trying to push yourself to a place where you don't even see yourself. You are constantly saying I can be beautiful! I can be beautiful! But you don't see yourself as beautiful. You constantly hear people say you are beautiful, but on the inside you feel that you look okay, but not really beautiful!

So being my own beautiful is not something I can say I have accomplished, but I strive to process that thought about my own self. I'm just striving and striving, and now that I have a daughter I want to make sure nothing changes her views about what I instill in her about her beauty. You may not have a small frame or light skin or small lips or small eyes, you might not have features that you perceive as beautiful, but you are beautiful . . . So I don't know, Devin.

B.Y.O.B.: Well, let me just go on the record to say that you are a very beautiful person on the outside as well as the inside, and I'm not just saying this to you, Destiny. I am a very up-front person, and what attracts me to you is your inside beauty. It makes you so much more beautiful on the outside. I promise you I would have never have come to you if I didn't think that you were a beautiful person, and you don't have to wear makeup every day; you have a natural beauty even though your look is unique . . . I talk about in the book, about rare beauty and how we all have it. I think that is what is beautiful about us. And even with myself, I was weighing almost three hundred pounds, and I couldn't stand to look at myself in the mirror and those who I thought were my friends were not helping—they would say, "Well, you are big." Why would you tell someone that if they already feel low about themselves? So when God began to deal with me about my inner beauty, he began to deal with me about my outer beauty. I remind myself every day, I get in the mirror and I say, "Devin, you are beautiful," and maybe at that moment I don't feel beautiful, but I tell myself that. I drill it in myself and in my heart. That is what I want to inspire other women to do because it's so important to feel that confidence within you. Destiny, you have really inspired me today. Thank you!

Destiny: No, thank you. You just ministered to me. No matter how many times we look in a mirror, we never see what other people see, and I wonder "Lord, why is that?" And you try to see what it is that they see, but you never will because I can't get into your mind and actually perceive what you see in me, so it is up to us to Be Our Own Beautiful—it's up to us. Because if we try to rely on other people, we won't be able to receive it because you need to know that you are beautiful within yourself. I love God to the point that if He doesn't do anything else for me, He has done enough. I'm glad He doesn't do things based upon the way I dress or look. He created us in His own image.

B.Y.O.B.: You know another thing that I'm learning is that I can't teach Destiny how to love Devin if Devin doesn't know how to love herself . . . and I believe in any relationship, it's a friendship—a relationship with your husband, sister, mother. If you can't love yourself, you can't teach them how to love you. So if I had a homegirl that came up to me and said, "Hey, B—" instead of using my name, I would stop her and say, "You know what, I don't even call myself that, so I would appreciate it if you didn't." That is a part of me loving myself and taking authority over how I want to be loved. So if you don't teach now them, then they have the right to love you the way they know how.

Devin Brown

Destiny: (With tears in her eyes.) As a child, I grew up with a lot of abandonment. I still deal with that today, with trust issues, so I know my struggles and that is half the battle. If I know what I'm struggling with then I know what I am fighting against. So I know what to pray for and stand up against. So dealing with the abandonment, I would hold on to abusive relationships because I'm used to abuse . . . Then I thought, "Wait a minute. This is not healthy for me," but I'm consistently holding on thinking, "If I let you go, I'm missing out on something but I just want you to love me. Please don't leave me; people are always leaving me that love me, from my father to my mother to my husband." It's like I could never get away from this to the point now I am stronger in that aspect than ever before, that is why I really had to grow closer to God because if I didn't, then I was on the verge of losing my mind. Losing it! And I know it was God. When I started traveling with Fred, all the hell and all the turmoil in my life to finally do something just stopped. The way the Fred Hammond gig came about, God just put me there with no effort of my own. I'm not calling, not asking how can I do First Lady Jakes, or asking where to send my résumé, I'm not doing any of that. All I'm doing is living for him . . . and in the midst of me living for him, people are trying to figure out why because he has constantly made my enemies my footstool. I don't use anyone to step on their head to get where I'm going. But when He (God) says "Yes, you have to go. I have made them your footstool so you have to step on their heads, you have to go . . ." God is telling you to go! It's like when a parent tells a child and a mother says, "What did I say? Don't worry about your friends, what did I tell you to do? Keep your eyes on me." And that is what God does, and that is what God has been doing to me and for me for five years now. This year alone has been blowing my mind and just between you and me, I pray that this book is to become highly blessed, not just to you, but I just want it to bless you to the point where so many people get a blessing through you. You're going to say, "Wait, how many people? A million? How did I do that?"

Devin Brown

How did this one person touch this many people, this one willing vessel, this one obedient child of mine—oh, she was so obedient to me.

B.Y.O.B.: Thank you. I receive it!

Destiny: I have cried many a night, and I have shed so many tears, but it is all worth it with Him (God); I have to keep going! I have lost so much, and been through so much but I keep going . . . I ask God sometimes when I am going to see the fruit of my labor. I don't have to touch it, but I just want to see it. But He won't show it to me, so we just have to keep going; if we stop, we fail. An idle mind can allow the enemy to call and take over and I can't allow that because he has had my mind and my body before. He even had me to the point where I didn't love myself anymore, to a point in time I tried to commit suicide plenty of times, but I am still here, I am still here by His grace. I was thinking about that earlier. And this book! Investing in this beauty, owning this beauty, being beautiful not only on the outside but on the inside. It's very much needed, especially for young girls, and even for women like me. (We share a laugh.) I need it too!

B.Y.O.B.: Yes! You know what I feel like. It starts young, and if it's not dealt with then it does develop in grown women.

Destiny, I appreciate you doing this for my book, and I pray that we can build a friendship . . . I feel privileged. Thank you.

Destiny: Absolutely! Thank you, Devin.

With tears still in her eyes, Destiny hugged me and we said our goodbyes for that day. We still keep in touch! She did my makeup for the cover of my book, *Be Your Own Beautiful*. And stay tuned for more work she and I will be doing! I'm so excited about the projects to come.

Devin Brown

FASHION AND MORE . . . .

INTERVIEW WITH:

K.Re'Nae

> The fashion of this world passeth away. 1 Corinthians 7:31

Born and raised in Dallas, Texas, K. Re'Nae grew up listening to a wide array of music. Her earliest memories of songwriting were when she was twelve years old, performing in a R&B girl group. Her musical gift was discovered at an early age while singing in church with her family. It's doubtful that her family knew that the timid girl would become a gospel powerhouse. She recalls, "When visiting my grandparents for the summer, my cousins and I opted to attend church with my grandfather, because church services were shorter there (my grandmother attended a Pentecostal church that started at eight am and ended around three pm). But God was up to something! At five years old, my grandfather began calling me up to sing 'We Are the World' every Sunday. Unknowingly, God was at work even then, setting the stage for what was to come."

Throughout the years, K. Re'Nae has had many accomplishments that would end up being vital parts of what God had planned from the very beginning. In her younger years, she continued to sing in various talent shows and school programs, but it wasn't until 1996 when, as a member of the South Oak Cliff High School Gospel Choir, she won the prestigious title of "Best Female Vocalist" in the Battle of the High School Choirs in Houston, Texas, and knew that her sole purpose in life was to minister the Gospel of Jesus Christ through music. At the age of seventeen she made a commitment to God to use her voice for His glory alone!

K. Re'Nae's ministry is about touching and making a difference in the lives of people who feel like there is no hope. With a heart and passion for God and desire for all to encounter the "full experience of life in Christ," this singer and songwriter counts it a privilege to spread the gospel of Jesus.

Devin Brown

K. Re'Nae's rich, honey-kissed tone draws in all who hear. Her debut album, *Life on Purpose,* reflects the variety of musical genres she has experienced, including Urban, Jazz, Neo-soul and even Rock. Most of the songs on *Life on Purpose* were written by K. Re'Nae in collaboration with her four producers: her brother, Kevin "St. Franks" Franklin, Amory Walker, and two other collaborators. Much of the album was recorded at a state-of-the-art home studio in Dallas, Texas, with Kevin Franklin, her brother, and cofounder of their independent label, Mansion Heights Music.

K. Re'Nae feels that her most rewarding accomplishment is the role she plays in her family. She is the daughter of the late Kenneth Franklin and Lu Martinez, and loving sister of three brothers and one sister, and the mother of one daughter, Dymon.

B.Y.O.B.:   I want to say thank you for coming to *mi casa* for this interview.

K. Re'Nae: No problem. Thanks for having me.

B.Y.O.B.:   What are some questions you ask someone to get them creatively thinking on how to find their fashion?

K. Re'Nae: The question would be who are you? And once you identify who you are then everything else should flow from that. If you appreciate eclectic—

B.Y.O.B.:   Before you go on, explain eclectic, please.

K. Re'Nae: Eclectic means off-center, against the grain—not quite the norm. Your own funky little flare.

B.Y.O.B.:   Oh, okay.

K. Re'Nae: If you like things that other people don't, then I don't expect you to be a classy-dress type of person because that is not your personality. But if you are very eccentric and you like African things and stone, you know, nature-type things, then I would expect more of that. So yes, the first question would be who are you? What is important to you? What types of things do you like? What colors do you like? What textures do you like? What tones do you like? What look are you trying to give off? How do you want to be perceived? And if you want to fit in, then something classy will work for you. If you want to go against the grain then something eclectic or eccentric will work for you. But you really need to identify who you are as a person first.

B.Y.O.B.: But, you know, like with me, since I have accomplished who I am on the inside, I want that to reflect on the outside. But I personally find it very hard to find my fashion sense. Like even if I go to a clothing store, it's like I know what I like, or if I see something in a magazine I will wear that, but I can't just go to the store and see something and just put this and that together and know that it's going to look right.

K. Re'Nae: The only thing I can say about this is that everyone is not a fashion-driven person; that is the first thing that needs to be identified. I think that fashion is a gift. I believe it's a sense of having an artistic gift; it's a work of art! So if you are not an artistic person and you are more of an intellectual person—you may not be able do that. So like you said, the best thing to do is to identify in books, magazines, online, pull up a look that you are trying to execute and say, "Okay, I like this look. This is where I am going to start. This will be my foundation." Then add *you* to that. To say I like this, but this element about this look I don't like, and I can change this or that to make it me, and I think that's another way if you are not good with fashion, or you're not good with colors to say that this works well with this. Not everyone has that gift to just put a look together. So I would just say mirror something that you like but just add you to it.

Devin Brown

B.Y.O.B.: Like even with me just personally, I like blazers (open or closed) with a maxi dress or a cami underneath with some jeans. I'm not a heel-wearing person, but I'm trying to get into that.

K. Re'Nae: I think there are five essential pieces that every woman should have: black slacks, white button-down shirt, a blazer of some kind, a pencil skirt or an A-line skirt (black or something neutral), and a casual shirt. From there, you add small little things to that. With those small pieces you can throw a colored shirt with a black pencil skirt and an off-color blazer. And you will be surprised that another can take that exact same outfit and the essential pieces and make it look totally different because of who they are and their personality.

B.Y.O.B.: So would it be safe to say that you can have more than one style?

K. Re'Nae: Most definitely. I'm a person who is a chameleon. I have had people stop me and tell me all the time, "Girl, you just keep people guessing. Every time I see you, you look totally different. You will see me on Monday with a high bun and nice and flowing clothes and very feminine, and then the very next day you will see me with something very edgy on. I will have my hair in a Mohawk and my makeup will be a little bolder; I will have big hoop earrings on. For me dressing, and this will sound crazy, but it's like role-playing. I will find a theme every day.

B.Y.O.B.: That's a good idea.

K. Re'Nae: Yes! It's according to how I feel. One day it's pop, the next day it's rock, and the next day urban. You have to do you according to how you feel.

B.Y.O.B.: So you definitely would have to work out of the box sometimes.

Devin Brown

K. Re'Nae: Most definitely! You always will have your signature look and that's good. Like me, I feel that I will always channel Kanisha.

B.Y.O.B.: Or K. Re'Nae. (Laughing.)

K. Re'Nae: Right. One day I might feel like Kanisha and the next K. Re'Nae, but it's always going to be me. You have to be open, that's the thing about art—it's an expression of who you are, how you feel.

B.Y.O.B.: So, tell us what you have on today. What were you feeling today? (Laughing.)

K. Re'Nae: Today I was tired (laughing) but I still wanted to do something nice. Today I would describe my outfit as eclectic chic; my hair is in a high bun. So I would say I stand out, even though I have on a maxi dress, with multicolor grays, greens, burgundy, with a black cardigan or shrug, and some gray wedges. I threw in a pop of color with some wooden bangles and wooden earrings.

B.Y.O.B.: That's what makes it earthy.

K. Re'Nae: Right! And my hair is up in a messy type of look but it's well put together, so it's eclectic but it has a chic look to it. So that's my look today with my makeup to complete it.

B.Y.O.B.: How big are you on color blocking?

K. Re'Nae: Color blocking is very trendy this year!

B.Y.O.B.: But I'm liking it!

K. Re'Nae: I like it too. But I try not to get into trends because I never want to look like anyone else! I do like the look.

B.Y.O.B.: You talked about your bangles and your earrings. How do you accessorize your outfit with your purses? Like with me, I wear the same jewelry every day with my necklace and my earrings. I guess I'm not too much out of the box like that, although I would like to get there.

K. Re'Nae: Right! I own about a hundred pieces of jewelry and every other weekend I go shopping for jewelry. I have my jewelry color-coded in a box. I have my bangles, my wood, and my metal. I really am into accessories. So for instance, with what I have on today the burgundy in this dress spoke to me this morning, so I thought, "Wow, I want to pull that out," and I got some burgundy earrings that match that pretty color.

B.Y.O.B.: Now do you think about that when you buy your jewelry? Do think "I have a dress that will match these."

K. Re'Nae: No! I don't ever buy outfits.

B.Y.O.B.: See I do that. Is that where I mess up? (Laughing.)

K. Re'Nae: Well, if that's how you process—

B.Y.O.B.: Well, that's the thing. I don't know.

K. Re'Nae: Well, as you can see, I'm not too matchy-matchy.

B.Y.O.B.: I have two questions in one. I have been around you for about four years now and I know that you are a very big bargain shopper. (We both laugh.) So where do you shop and how do you bargain shop?

K. Re'Nae: Bargain shopper is pretty self-explanatory—I go in with a budget that I will not go over, period. My shoes I will not go over twenty dollars. There may be a pair of shoes that I may just have to get that's over twenty dollars, but I can count on one hand how many times that has happened in two or three years.

B.Y.O.B.: Really! You have a lot of shoes because I have been in your closet, and they don't look like they cost less than twenty dollars.

K. Re'Nae: No, there is a way to get quality for cheap—I believe in quality! One of my favorite places to shop is the Half of Half store; they sell BCG jeans, Donna Karan, and any name brand you can think of. I have an eye for good, quality things. There can be a rack full of clothes and this one quality piece of clothing can be smashed in between everything else . . . but I know quality. I will spend nine and ten dollars on a pair of BCG jeans; I have pieces that were three and four hundred dollars, and I only spent twenty-nine dollars. I refuse to spend full price on anything.

B.Y.O.B.: I have been to Half of Half and I can never find anything—I guess you have to have patience for it.

K. Re'Nae: And an eye. My friends and I will go to Half of Half together and they come up with nothing and I will have a handful of stuff and would have gone down the same aisle. And they want to know how I found that? My answer to that will be I have an eye for it; I look at the way something hangs and know that it's going to be cute on . . . I just have an eye for fashion.

B.Y.O.B.: So besides Half of Half what other stores do you shop at?

K. Re'Nae: Rue21. I recently started shopping there because they have really good clearance racks.

(We both laugh.)

K. Re'Nae: They do! This weekend I saved about 247 dollars.

Devin Brown

B.Y.O.B.: I'm sorry, did you say *save*?

K. Re'Nae: Yes, saved. I spent eighty and saved 247.

B.Y.O.B.: Really!

K. Re'Nae: Yes, I got five or six outfits for Dymon, my daughter, and then I got about twelve shirts for myself.

B.Y.O.B.: For eighty dollars?

K. Re'Nae: Yes, for eighty dollars! I wish I had the receipt to show you, but I took it out of my purse. But I also shop at Forever 21. I usually don't shop at the malls because they are usually overpriced, but for some jewelry and clothes I will go there. I love good clothes and it doesn't have to be name brand—I am not a label person. I can buy something for five dollars and I can make it look like a million.

B.Y.O.B.: (Laughing.) I am so enjoying your confidence. (We both laugh.)

K. Re'Nae: It's not my confidence in me; it's confidence of knowing how to put things together.

B.Y.O.B.: I know you said earlier that it's a gift and that you have to have an eye for it, but can it be learned?

K. Re'Nae: I believe it's a gift—if it was not a gift then people wouldn't seek out personal shoppers.

B.Y.O.B.: Well, I am definitely learning and that's why I am doing this segment in my book. Not only for me, but for my B.Y.O.B. readers.

K. Re'Nae: Can I interject, because I don't want it to sound egotistical . . . I don't! But just like you—you are a writer and I am not. I don't write at all and I don't enjoy writing;

Devin Brown

there is nothing that draws me to it. I can read someone's book and think "Wow, this is a well-written book," but it's not something that I am gifted in.

B.Y.O.B.: Right!

K. Re'Nae: So does that make it egotistical for me to say you can't do this like I can . . . No, it doesn't! It's your gift—that is why God gives all different gifts, because we are all needed. If we all are able to do the same thing, then we wouldn't find the value in each other. So I have a gift in fashion and you have a gift in writing. I just believe that it is necessary and that's why we value each other.

B.Y.O.B.: You don't sound egotistical (laughing), but I have to say when I get ready to do my photo shoot for my book, you're going to have to go shopping with me.

K. Re'Nae: And I will!

B.Y.O.B.: (Laughing.) Especially if we get clothes for cheap.

K. Re'Nae: That I can do. You will be cute and still have change in your pocket!

B.Y.O.B.: Okay! I'm looking forward to that.

B.Y.O.B.: Do you think it is okay to judge someone by the way they dress?

K. Re'Nae: I don't think it is! I truly don't, because just like me or anyone else—I'm not you and I don't know anything about your story. And I have to respect the way you dress and who you are as an individual and know that we are two different people and you have the right to be you. You owe it to yourself to be you, and why would I look down on a person, or judge a person? A person doesn't have to take on another personality, so why would it bother you? It's important that you do you and let them do them. I just believe in people being individuals.

B.Y.O.B.: I agree!

K. Re'Nae: I also want to say my job title is considered a low grade by the people I work with. I work with a lot of executives and I have a lot of people come up to me and say, "Oh, I thought you were in management," because I don't dress by what I make necessarily. But the people that know me and know that I am just an administrator to a director ask me, "How do you do it? How do you find the money to shop?" As if I'm not privileged to a certain look based on what I make.

B.Y.O.B.: What they are doing is passing judgment.

K. Re'Nae: Right! And that's why it's wrong. And there is a flip side to it; I see people respect me more because they think I am management.

B.Y.O.B.: To add to that, and I talk about it early on in my book, if you see yourself as management they hang around those who are managers and dress like one.

K. Re'Nae: Absolutely! And that is why I outdress my boss.

(We both laugh.)

K. Re'Nae: As his administrator . . . and now he wears ties and nice shirts, whereas he used to wear polo shirts and slacks.

B.Y.O.B.: Who or what inspires you to be as creative as you are? What inspires you, because you are definitely inspiring other people.

K. Re'Nae: This is going to sound so . . . but it is what it is. But I inspire me.

Devin Brown

B.Y.O.B.: No, that is good . . . (Laughing.)

K. Re'Nae: I know that sounds bad.

B.Y.O.B.: No, it really doesn't . . . that lets me know that you have a love for yourself.

K. Re'Nae: Yes I do! I can remember back as far as sixth grade, and I don't know if you remember Bell Biv Devoe (BBD)?

B.Y.O.B.: Yes, I do!

K. Re'Nae: On what video—I think it was Poison—but they had one pants leg short and one long, and I made my own. And I made them for the whole "hood." I had the paint and everything. All I have to do is watch something once, and I can do it and create it to be my own. So I inspire me. And if I see something on someone else that I think is cute and they are walking by I will stop them and compliment them on it, because I believe in uplifting each other instead of turning my nose up at somebody else and saying I like it, but . . . I can give compliments because I love me. And I can respect other's individuality.

B.Y.O.B.: I do know people like that. I could compliment people all day long, and say, "Your hair is so pretty," but when I come in with my hair done, it's "who did your hair," and "girl, you think your hair is cute?" It's always something negative. And personally I think that it's hate. In the front part of the book I talk about the "crab syndrome"—pulling others down while you are trying to get to the top. But you never get to the top because it's always going to come back around and somebody will always be there to pull you down. I don't understand us as women and why we can't help uplift other women—let's all make it to the top.

K. Re'Nae: I have so many people around me, my personal friends. I will not allow a person to be around me without being better. I don't want you to be where I am or where you were when you first met me. That is the mentality people have—if you are a little bit below or under me then we are cool. But if you get where I am or a little bit higher, then now I am hating. No! What I want to do is be able to pour into you. I want you to be better than me, because I can get better if I am with the best. If I feel as though I am the best then that means that I have arrived—I have excelled and there is nowhere else for me to go. So I'm always adding to others.

B.Y.O.B.: Because I, myself, have come to you and taken your tips and applied them to make them my own.

K. Re'Nae: Right! And that is what we are supposed to do, each one teaches one . . . because I had to learn from somewhere. I just believe in sharing . . . let's share the wealth!

B.Y.O.B.: I agree! What is the most common fashion mistake people make? I know we stated before that people have their own style.

K. Re'Nae: This is my personal opinion—but the first one would be being a carbon copy of someone. This is a big fashion no-no; you can never execute someone else's look, ever. That is the biggest fashion mistake, and that's not being you. Second would be wearing something that you are not comfortable with. If you can pull something off with confidence, then you can wear whatever you want. You're a big girl and you can walk with your head up high and you are truly compatible with what you have on, because confidence sells . . .

B.Y.O.B.: It does!

K. Re'Nae: Everything . . . confidence sells everything. You can be a small girl with the body to work with and have on a dress, but you're always tugging at it . . . you have the body to carry it but you don't have the confidence to carry it.

B.Y.O.B.: I always say a woman can't wear anything more beautiful than her confidence.

K. Re'Nae: You are absolutely correct! I believe wearing something that you are not confident in is a no-no. I would also say wearing something that you can't fit in is also a fashion don't. Pants, skirts, shirts—muffin tops are real. (We both laugh.) You can be a size one and wearing a zero and you are going to have a muffin top, so find your size and find what works for you. Find what works well with your body. I know for me, I am a little heavier in the midsection, so baby-doll style works well on me because I have a small chest and I don't have hips, so I can wear something A-line (narrow at the top and flared at the bottom)—that works well for me because I have more of an apple shape. So it's important to know your body so that you can find and wear things that accentuate your strong points.

B.Y.O.B.: Since I have been learning about my body and what looks good on me, I have found out that skinny jeans look good on me. And I have found what works for me, and it feels good to know what flatters my body.

K. Re'Nae: That is what I'm talking about. Find out what works for you and build off that.

B.Y.O.B.: It's like sometimes you're going to fall, but get back up because if you keep trying you will found out who you are.

K. Re'Nae: That is right, because knowing is half the battle.

B.Y.O.B.: Right!

B.Y.O.B.: Your hair is natural, which means you have no perm.

Devin Brown

K. Re'Nae: No chemicals.

B.Y.O.B.: Yes! So what made you want to go natural, because you had perms before?

K. Re'Nae: The reason why I went natural is because my daughter didn't want to get relaxer anymore. And she's been asking me for years, because she hated the chemical burns. In June 2009 was our last relaxer, and that was three years ago.

B.Y.O.B.: So your daughter pretty much inspired you to go natural?

K. Re'Nae: Yes, my daughter is the reason I began to start wearing braids and then I decided after six months of growing my relaxer out to cut my hair off.

B.Y.O.B.: Yes, I remember! You can't tell now that you cut your hair.

K. Re'Nae: People called me crazy, called me nappy head, asking me what I was doing and this was before natural was popular, as it is now. It was not a trend. At the time I was going natural you were getting talked about. I did it because my daughter didn't want relaxers anymore.

B.Y.O.B.: So in spite of being talked about, you decided to do you.

K. Re'Nae: Yes, I did. I decided to Be My Own Beautiful. And I have to give props to my daughter, Dymon, because she decided to cut her hair off after nine months of not having a perm, and she is in the sixth grade, so she is among all these children who are used to long hair. She was asked why she cut her hair and why didn't she get a perm (because her hair was short and kinky) and she nicely told them, "Because I like it." She wasn't ugly about it, but she was very confident. And I ask her all the time now she is going to high school, "Are you sure you don't want to perm your hair," and she tells me no.

Devin Brown

B.Y.O.B.: Well, I myself am not natural, but I know some of my B.Y.O.B. readers (Rare Beauties) are natural. What type of products do you use on your hair?

K. Re'Nae: I use the cheap products. (We share a laugh.) Just like my clothes. I spend twenty dollars every six months on hair products. Suave conditioner, which is two dollars and sixty-eight cents, Ego styling gel, and I use Giovanni direct leave-in, which is an organic leave-in conditioner. At your Whole Foods you can buy it for seven dollars, but I buy it directly online at a massage warehouse for twelve dollars and it lasts me for six to eight months. And water . . . That is all I use on my hair.

B.Y.O.B.: Your hair is naturally curly.

K. Re'Nae: It is!

B.Y.O.B.: I love it, and all the styles that you rock.

K. Re'Nae: Thank you! I have grown my hair for three months and wear it natural. It has caused it to grow fast; my hair is down my back.

B.Y.O.B.: It is, and you cut it short, like a taper fade.

K. Re'Nae: Yes, I did!

B.Y.O.B.: You said earlier that going natural is a trend, so what do you do to set yourself apart from that trend?

K. Re'Nae: The one thing I can say about being natural is there are no two heads that are the same, period! My texture isn't going to be anything like the next. That's the beauty of natural hair. I just do me, I go from a fro to a ponytail to a twist-out, or straight if I want to throw color in my hair.

B.Y.O.B.: I talked about idolizing in my book. I had a definition of **_Idolize_**: to regard with blind admiration or devotion, to worship as an idol. So how do you handle a person who comes to you for advice? I have a lot of people that come to me for advice, too. So what I am trying to ask is how do you deal with others that come to you out of admiration but don't know how to take what you give them and make it their own? Instead, they become a carbon copy. Earlier on in my book I called it theft. It's a type of identity theft, if you are carbon copying someone then you are not being you, and you are putting yourself in a prison—there is no freedom within yourself. I wanted to talk about this because it is so crucial amongst women—it can cause death from the inside. So how would you explain to someone that is reading this how to admire something from someone but still do it their own way so they are staying true to themselves?

K. Re'Nae: This is a very sensitive subject to me, and I will start off by saying something that dropped in my spirit: I am a woman of God and more than anything I take things back to the word of God. When you talked about idolizing, in the Bible it talks about not putting another god before Me (God). We were not made to esteem anything higher than God, and if you can't appreciate what God has given you, and if you can't appreciate what God has made you, you will never live up to what God has called you to be. Like you said before, it is suicide; you have killed your identity. And you are basically telling God "What you gave me is not good enough, so I am going to mirror someone else!" It's self-hatred, not liking who you are so you copy this person because you feel that who you are is not good enough for the world to see. When you truly love yourself, you see your value and what you have to offer, and you want to share that and extend what you have. If you keep "you" hidden by another person's image, how would you have been seen? How would you ever be taken seriously? That's why people walk around hating, because they are not happy with themselves and they are in prison. Think about some prisoners: they are mad, angry, and act out with bad behavior. Similarly, if you have someone on the inside dying to be seen and freed, the only way you know how to express that is hate.

B.Y.O.B.:   Wow! That is so true. Misery loves company!

K. Re'Nae: It does, but you know what? You can't keep love down. You can't, no matter how much hate you put toward someone; if they truly love themselves, you can't keep them down. Also, just because you don't know who you are and decided to mirror someone else, that doesn't mean someone else can't see you. They may walk up to you and think "that's not you—hmmm, you're looking like Kanisha today." (We share a laugh.) But they know me and I know me because my identity is out there. So people are able to put two and two together and say that looks more like this person. So you can never accomplish what you're trying to do by copying someone else, so that's why you are frustrated and you start hating.

B.Y.O.B.:   That is my own reason for writing *Be Your Own Beautiful*. I am so passionate about this. Because for me it wasn't with clothes, but on the inside I'd mimic or seek validation from someone else. Even when I was in a room full of people, I still felt by myself. And this starts young—that's how bullying comes about! But I believe this book can help. I mean, it's a lot of soul-searching. I use a phrase in my book, "Inspire others by simply being you." When I started looking at Devin, there were times I stopped and said, "I don't like that about myself."

K. Re'Nae: That's why people can't make it past that, because you have to first identify that you are an "ugly" person. And see the things that you do that aren't so pretty . . . and like you said, start working from the inside out and once you do that, then you will be able to love and accept you and before you know it . . . the word of God says love covers a world of multitude, so if you begin to love yourself all those other things that come from that hatred, they begin to be replaced by love.

B.Y.O.B.: And it becomes you, because it's so natural and it's not hard. Now it's not hard for me to love somebody, but at one point I had so much anger I always wanted to fight. But I really do appreciate you doing this interview because I want my readers to be well-rounded and work from the inside out, so this segment will help with the fashion. I also want them to learn and be inspired as well as me, because this is where I am now: I'm working on the outside.

B.Y.O.B.: And you are in Dallas, Texas. So what do you have going for yourself?

K. Re'Nae: I am working on my personal album. It is called *Out of the Saltshaker*, meaning that God has called us to be the salt and light of the Earth and if we hold our gifts in a saltshaker where people are never able to see them, then how can we be the flavor that we are supposed to be? So it's me releasing what I have tried to have control of and actually come out of the saltshaker and into the world. It doesn't have a release date yet. But I also have a T-shirt line that I am working on as well.

B.Y.O.B.: Do you have a website or a blog?

K. Re'Nae: I have a video blog on YouTube. It is KRENAE4christ. I also have a Facebook page for natural hair called Kurl Friends Konnection. It has styles and tips from me, and also tips from other people.

B.Y.O.B.: Thank you so much. Again, I appreciate you being a part of this project.

K. Re'Nae: I really want to say this—I pray that you really prosper in what you are doing, and His hand is already on this because it's edifying and that's what He called us to do, to build each other up, and I feel that what you are trying to do is a calling from God. I believe that you are being the salt and the light of the Earth. I pray that God gives you provision and everything that you need to open every door concerning this project that you are doing.

B.Y.O.B.: Thank you so much! I receive it!

B.Y.O.B.: Before we go, can you sum up the phrase Be Your Own Beautiful?

K. Re'Nae: Be Your Own Beautiful—be you! Be the best that you can be. It's impossible to be anyone else's best, so be *your* best!

B.Y.O.B.: So, you guys, go check her out and tell her B.Y.O.B. sent you!

INTERVIEW WITH:

Stephanie Long

(Fashionista—she styles you)

"Style is a way to say who you are without having to speak."

Stephanie Long

I am a Freelance Fashion Stylist. I was born and raised in Hollywood, Florida. I am a happily married woman of eighteen years to a soldier in the Army. I am a proud mother of two beautiful daughters, ages eighteen and eleven. I have had an opportunity to travel the world as a military wife.

As a child, I always took pride in my appearance. I was fortunate to be raised by a strong single mother of four daughters and a village of confident, beautiful, and fashion-forward women. My love for fashion started as far back as I can remember, at the age of five. I have always been creative and style savvy.

Although I have not had any formal education in fashion, I have worked for companies that have informally educated me on the aspects of running a successful clothing store. I have sixteen years of retail management experience with companies such as Regis Corp., Express, Charlotte-Russe, and New York & Company.

My dream has always been to open my own chain of consignment boutique shops across the world. My mission is to get women to start loving themselves! I grew up in a home where my mother was "fly" every time she stepped out. As a daughter, I was proud to say, "That's my mama." I learned at a young age to love myself. I feel like fashion repeats itself, so why not make fashion affordable and accessible to the average woman? Beyoncé says it best: "God made her, however she likes to think, and she was created." My thoughts exactly!

God blessed me with daughters for a reason. I felt I should have already opened the boutique years ago, but God said I wasn't ready. I have been blessed with beautiful "living dolls." We have played dress up, had photo shoots, and a love affair with fashion that bonds us. My girls have developed their own sense of style and they "own" it. We have raised them to love themselves and to know their worth. God made me wait for them to mature, to take part in building our family legacy, EclecticNistas. The legacy is to share with the world our love for style, beauty and self-worth.

B.Y.O.B.: Thank you for taking the time out to participate in Be Your Own Beautiful for our readers and thank you for allowing me to interview you for my book.

Stephanie: You're welcome!

B.Y.O.B.: How did you get into styling and fashion?

Stephanie: Even as a young girl I always had to have the fly stuff and be very different and stand out. I had some cousins that were in a little-girl singing group and when I was in high school I would sit outside and help them practice and help them with their choreography and also tell them how to wear their outfits. From that point their mom would say we would go and pick out your clothes and outfits and they would say, "No, we don't want you to pick them out. We want Stephanie to pick them out." I would say the idea and doing the act of styling and love of styling started at the age of eleven or twelve.I just like helping other people dress themselves and put stuff together because some people just don't know.

B.Y.O.B.:   Exactly. I'm probably one of those—I feel like fashion is such an art, and not everybody is gifted with that.

Stephanie: That's true. My husband went to the thrift store with me once and asked me if I was crazy when I told him how long I planned on staying. He said it overwhelmed him just walking in the door, but I always feel like I'm on a treasure hunt. I just have an eye for it—I don't have to walk down every aisle and go through every piece of clothing. I just walk by and if I see a nice print or design I snatch it down and it's in my cart. He said I have such an eye for it because there is no way he would have thought I would have come out of the store with half the stuff I did.

B.Y.O.B.:   Absolutely.

Stephanie: I have fun with it.

B.Y.O.B.:   Yeah, you have to have that gift because for me just going to the thrift store or Ross or anything like that and having to search—I don't have the patience for it.

Stephanie: It can be overwhelming.

B.Y.O.B.:   It certainly can. How do you update yourself with the latest trends and fashions that are on the market?

Stephanie: That's so simple. Literally, fashion repeats itself. Every spring it's going be a nautical theme that comes out; every fall, men's wear comes out. I have such a collection of clothing it's not even funny. I think we went over our weight with our move because of my wardrobe. I update mine by constantly reading magazines. My favorite magazine is *Style* by *People*. My children know not to open the seal on that magazine until I see it; they know this. I read a lot of magazines and I read a lot of fashion books. My favorite designer is Chanel and I like her collection just because she is classic—black and white, timeless—all you have to do is just add things to make it trendier with her. As far as updating my own wardrobe, I basically can just use what I have. It's just revamping your wardrobe. Sometimes you don't have to go out shopping to be in the latest trend, you can have it right in your closet already—you just have to know how to work it.

B.Y.O.B.: That's interesting. Okay, I was looking on your Facebook page and you have just won me over with the jumpers.

Stephanie: Oh my God, girl, I've been collecting them for over ten years and before they became popular in the past year and a half. I was already on that game. That is the easiest outfit; it's just like a maxi dress, and when you need to go somewhere and you need to get cute quick, then let's talk. Everyone needs to have their go-to dress. You can just throw it on and depending on where you're going and what time it is, and be good to go.

B.Y.O.B.: I'm not sure how I would look in a jumpsuit. I'm going to have to go and find one and just try it on because you really have me curious about them.

Stephanie: That's all it is. When you go in the stores, don't judge something by how it looks on a hanger—the hanger doesn't have curves and it isn't breathing. Obviously you have to literally go in that dressing room and try it on. And come out feeling like you've been missing out. See, that's how you're feeling right now, like you need to try this.

B.Y.O.B.: Exactly, I really do. I'm thinking the next time I go shopping I'm going to find a jumper, because you have me curious about it. The ones you have look really nice and the pictures you have been posting make the simple look of them really cute.

Stephanie: You would be shocked what a belt can do to an outfit, or a simple dinner jacket, or denim vest, or make it a little edgy—throw on a leather motorcycle jacket or a leopard jacket. Just adding an accessory like that can change the entire look of your outfit.

B.Y.O.B.: Wow, so I will definitely have to go and try one on! I am still trying to find my fashion sense, but I have realized that I look very good in skinny jeans.

Stephanie: So you feel confident in skinny jeans?

B.Y.O.B.: Yes, I do!

Stephanie: I'll tell you what—tomorrow the topic I post will be about skinny jeans and how to wear them.

B.Y.O.B.: (Laughing.) Okay.

Stephanie: So you can have some visuals and if you see something that you like, let me know and I'll try to find it. You know, times have changed so much, and there are so many great stores with great fashion. You don't have to be a size four to look good—you can be a plus size and look just as good. My blog does not just cater to one size; we all come in different shapes, sizes, and colors. I love to see a plus-size woman with confidence—you can't tell her that she's not owning it. I love to see that!

B.Y.O.B.: I love that you have so much passion for fashion and that you love to help others and see that confidence come to life! And it's clear that you have an eye for fashion.

Stephanie: I am seeking to understand why in today's world no one wants to give anyone a chance in this industry. This is what I love to do—so much that I have offered my services for free to get my foot in the door. But God is showing me something every day and that is that I am heading in the right direction. I had a friend that I went to high school with and she emailed me asking me if I could help her daughter out, who is interested in fashion. I told her that I would be more than happy to show her daughter, even though people have not wanted to show me the way, but I would be more than willing to. That is going to be the difference with me—I am going to share it.

B.Y.O.B.: You are a person who loves to inspire! And it really should be a domino effect so when she learns from you, then she should be willing to share that same teaching and want to inspire someone else. So I think that is awesome. But time has changed and people have changed, and I don't understand why for the life of me why people don't want to see others grow.

Stephanie: Me either, but I have promised myself that I will not be that person. And what I want to do is not even on a celebrity level. I wouldn't mind working with celebrities. But to me there are average, everyday women that are not in the spotlight and get lost in the world and they don't know how to find themselves.

B.Y.O.B.: How would you describe your signature look?

Stephanie: Well, my name says it all: EclecticNista; I am a fashionista and a lover of all fashion from all eras. I dress depending on my mood; my wardrobe is very eclectic! It consists of a lot of vintage. I like the mall but that is not my favorite place to shop. I like the thrift stores and such! And I know my measurements too. (We share a laugh.) I really do, so I will pull out a measuring tape real quick.

B.Y.O.B.: Can you look out at someone and know their measurements?

Stephanie: Some people! Depending on what they are wearing, because sometimes people hide behind their clothing. They think they are camouflaging, but in reality it makes them look bigger than they really are. I used to work with a young lady who I saw out of uniform and I didn't know she had a shape until then. I mean, she was shaped like a Coca-Cola bottle. I told her she was fine (we laugh), but you could never tell because of how she wore her clothes. I told her she needed to change up her style and I helped her.

B.Y.O.B.: That's something that we as women don't even realize: wearing big clothes makes us look bigger than what we really are. I used to do that and sometimes still do, so that's good that you were able to help her.

Stephanie: Yes. I also would like to open up my own shop. I do a lot of shopping, and this a true story. I rarely wear something twice; it's got to be something I feel so fly in for me to keep. But other than that, I wear it once and get my moment out of it and then it goes to the closet to be collected, so I want to be able to open a shop and resell my own clothes.

B.Y.O.B.: So are you close to that; have you been looking at places?

Stephanie: Yes. That's actually my next step, since I have my Facebook fan page up now. I used to do eBay—I am an eBay addict. But I am going to start selling on there again. I had a great eBay clientele. I just moved here though, so I'm looking at locations.

B.Y.O.B.: Well, when you get open and start your eBay shop, let me know. I know you are smaller than me but I may be able to find something to squeeze in. (We laugh.)

Stephanie: You said you're a work in progress, so you never know.

B.Y.O.B.: What are your favorite trends this season?

Stephanie: The high-low styles! High-low dress, shirt, and skirts—you name it, I like it.

B.Y.O.B.: Yeah, those are cute. I've seen a few of them you posted on your fan page.

Stephanie: High-low dresses, and I'm a lover of jumpers! As for as accessories, I'm loving the scarves and the funky turbans. I stepped out of the house a couple of weeks ago to get my nails done and my husband was surprised I was wearing a scarf outside, and I asked him, "Do you see these earrings? (We laugh.) Yes! I'm wearing this scarf." I thought I was cute. As far as shoes, I am a huge fan of the open-toe pumps and wedges. Open-toe pumps make your feet and your legs look really sexy. It's the toe cleavage you get from the open toe. (Laughing.) Yes, but those are my favorites this season!

B.Y.O.B.: Yeah, those are my favorite types of shoes as well when I have to dress up!

B.Y.O.B.: What is a trend that you'd like to see go away?

Stephanie: Hmmm. Well, this is not a particular clothing trend and it has to do with the male aspect, and it's the sagging. It's a real failing to see a grown man do it.

B.Y.O.B.: It's a turn-off.

Stephanie: Yes! A serious one! And that lets me know you have not matured or grown. I had a guy that opened the door for me one day and he was sagging, but I thought, "Okay sugar still exists." He asked what that meant and I told him he is too grown for that.

B.Y.O.B.: I hope you inspired him to stop sagging. (Laughing.)

Stephanie: I do too. That is one trend that I wish would go away and never ever come back. My husband has told my daughter that she better not ever bring a guy to our house with his pants hanging off his butt, because he will turn him right back around. (Laughing.) There is no class in it; I don't care if they are wearing designer jeans . . . there's just no class.

B.Y.O.B.: That is the truth. So what or who inspires you?

Stephanie: I believe when you look good, you feel good on the inside and out. I even believe (this might sound weird) but when women have matched set of panties and bra I think a woman feels sexier. I feel like my inspiration comes from my mother. Growing up, my mother was a fly woman. I used to always say, "When I grow up, I want to be just like her." Even when we're together today she'll say, "Steph, when I get around you I got to step my swag up." (Laughing.) She always tells me I get it from her but do it better. And I tell her I learned from the best and advanced my skills. I use everything around me to my advantage, from my job on down. I worked at Cracker Barrel for six years, and I had a group of friends and they had a group called the Fly Big Girls, and they told me that I was their little mascot because I inspired them.

B.Y.O.B.: I think that is awesome that you have inspired a group of women like that! That says a lot about you and your character and the way you dress.

B.Y.O.B.: What is the most important advice you can give?

Stephanie: This is kind of funny, but my friend went into H&M and they are a European store, and she is a size four. I told her not to go in there until she got her true size—she will need to go up two sizes. She did just that—she gets her size, which is a size four. So she calls me and tells me that I was right; she couldn't even get her arm through the sleeve. (We laugh.) So my advice would be don't hold on to your size; don't just look at the numbers. You need to know if you put it on if it's going to fit you properly. Wear clothes that fit. The numbers (size) are not that serious. (Laughing.)

B.Y.O.B.: It's funny how we women have pride in that area!

B.Y.O.B.: Do you have any beauty secrets to share?

Stephanie: Yes, I do—it will be the Vaseline body gel oil. Mix it with your favorite lotion and I always add a little bronze powder to my Vaseline gel, so I will always have a little glow. You will be so moisturized and you will be glowing. It's a sexy look! (We share a laugh.)

B.Y.O.B.: That's good! Because we can put lotion on and then get ashy within the next hour or two, especially around the ankle. (We laugh.) And you never know who is looking at you, so it's good to always be on point even with your skin (laughing), so that's good!

B.Y.O.B.: What is your favorite thing in your closet? I know that's hard for you to just pick one. (We laugh.)

Stephanie: It is, but I will keep it simple. It's a pair of jeans—my go-to jeans. I own twelve pair of them. (Laughing.) Seven For All Mankind jeans—if you want something similar to that, they have some at the Gap made for curvy women. They are cheaper, but they are comparable.

B.Y.O.B.: Really! I will look into that. I like learning about clothes because I am still a beginner. (Laughing.) I will do my research on that!

B.Y.O.B.: You travel a lot because of your husband being in the military. Where are some of your favorite places in the world to shop?

Stephanie: New York! It is so much fun, I feel like a kid in a candy shop . . . (Laughing.) And I have a second place in Ireland. The shopping there was awesome!

B.Y.O.B.: I hear Ireland is a beautiful place, by the way!

Stephanie: It is! It's a place where you can experience all four seasons in one day!

B.Y.O.B.: Wow, how interesting is that!

B.Y.O.B.: So who would you say qualifies to be a true fashion icon?

Stephanie: Coco Chanel. I have seen her movies and am just blown away at how she was able to set herself aside from all the women in that time, and how she was able to streamline her look from the pilgrim-like dress and hooped skirts to her tailor-made dresses with bows and flowers. She had a swag all of her own—she took something so basic but she added a sexy twist to it. I like the fact that you can be sexy and not show all your goodies.

B.Y.O.B.: What styling tips do you have for teens?

Stephanie: Be yourself. It is that simple; you don't have to be a follower. My daughter just graduated high school and she has always had her own style. I have watched her grow and change, and I am pleased with the young lady that she has become. I get really emotional talking about it. She went to a high school where she wasn't around people of her ethnicity, and she was definitely in the minority and it put a strain on her. And this is where I get emotional, because she was a cheerleader for her sophomore and junior year and kids can be so rude. She would get questions like "do you sunburn?" Things like that upset her—it got so bad she didn't want to cheer her senior year. Her father and I got so fed up with it when she took this class in school called Social Psychology. They were discussing real-life situations, and her teacher asked her "How does it feel when you see a biracial couple?"

B.Y.O.B.: What kind of question is that? That's a form of bullying!

Stephanie: It is! I asked her what was her response, and she said she told the woman, "Why don't you call my mother, and why don't you ask her?" I don't understand why you would ask a child something like that. But children can be so mean, even in elementary. With my youngest child, my husband saw her diary and he didn't want to be nosy or anything, but of course he had to open it and found out that she had a little crush on a little boy. You really don't know how children feel, but the little boy ended up liking someone else and my daughter didn't think she was pretty enough. So my husband let her know that she was beautiful and for her not to let anyone define who she is. You have to tap into your kids and their self-esteem early on because if you don't, someone will come and destroy it.

B.Y.O.B.: That is so true, and it's so sad that children have to go through such harsh things from their peers.

B.Y.O.B.: Whose closet would you like to raid?

Stephanie: It's not just one. (Laughing.) It's three in particular because I'm eclectic, remember? (Laughing.) Okay, it would have to be Sarah Jessica Parker, Kim Kardashian, and Jennifer Lopez.

B.Y.O.B.: Really! (Laughing) You would have a field day!

Stephanie: Yes, I would. If I ever have to perform on stage I would have to hit Beyoncé's closet. (Laughing.)

B.Y.O.B.: Who would you say your dream client would be?

Devin Brown

Stephanie: Beyoncé would be at the top of the list; I would love to work with her. Lady Gaga—people really do sleep on her. And I believe Lady Gaga would give me creative freedom. And Jennifer Hudson—she went from Effie to fabulous. (Laughing.) She looks great!

B.Y.O.B.: What approach do you take to communicate with clients? How do you get that picture to know what it is they are looking for?

Stephanie: I like to ask a client to show up in what they consider their best, and once I see what their best is, then it's my duty to show them how to polish it up. So take what they want and what they consider their best and help them merge it.

B.Y.O.B.: When you hear "Be Your Own Beautiful," what does that mean to you?

Stephanie: It means exactly that: Be Your Own Beautiful. You don't have to be Beyoncé or Halle Berry, and you don't have to be anybody else but yourself. It's about loving and falling in love with you.

B.Y.O.B.: I so agree. Stephanie, thanks so much for being a part of this. You have inspired me in fashion and to have patience with myself when it comes to shopping. Take it from a plus-size girl, shopping wasn't on my list of favorite things to do. Where can readers reach you?

Stephanie: Like my Facebook fan page: EclecticNista.

B.Y.O.B.: Thanks again!

INTERVIEW WITH:

Amanda Armon

"Pain is the weakness leaving your body."

-Daniel R. Evans

Interview with Amanda Armon

Personal Trainer

Amanda Armon is a graduate from the University of North Texas, majoring in Health Promotion. Amanda has received certifications in group exercise and personal training.

In high school, Amanda was into cosmetology and had always wanted to be in the hair industry since she could remember. After getting her license to do hair, she had an apprenticeship in The Woodlands, Texas, for over a year, but then she found out that her dad's job was transferring him to Dallas, Texas. Amanda jumped on the opportunity to go to Dallas, not knowing if she wanted to stay in the hair industry or go back to school. When the move finally came, Amanda put her shears down and enrolled in community college. Amanda started to get into fitness and health and thought that was her calling. After two years in community college, Amanda transferred to University of North Texas and began to pursue her health promotion degree. While she was in college, she taught group-exercise classes to help her gain more experience in her field. After three years at UNT, she graduated in 2009.

In 2010, she began her career in corporate fitness, where she now works as a trainer and also a group-exercise instructor.

"I love every bit of my job. I get to work with all kinds of individuals and learn so much about them, being able to see people transform their bodies and view of health and life is such a joy. I love that I have inspired people and continue to do so."

Devin Brown

B.Y.O.B.:   Why did you become a fitness professional?

Amanda: In college I would take group classes at the gym, because sometimes I needed an extra push in my workouts, and the treadmill got to be a little boring. Well, I got to be a regular in certain classes and one of the teachers came up to me and told me that I could and should be teaching my own classes. The next month I signed up for training, got my certification, and taught classes through college. When I came to work for this company we didn't offer training for a while and then we got it approved. People were so excited to finally get a personal trainer.

I enjoy training because you are helping people change their lives. You are pushing them to their goals and you are seeing their life and body change. I always tell my clients that it starts off hard, but then it will get easier. But when it gets easier, I then push you more! Everyone is different and we all have to start somewhere.

B.Y.O.B.:   What kind of questions do you ask a client before training them and why?

Amanda: I ask them what are their goals and what are they looking to get out of this. Most women, for example—women always want to tone their stomach, legs, and arms. They always say "I want a six-pack; I want this lifted and toned." Well you just can't do a million crunches to achieve a six-pack; it takes time and a lot of work and dedication to be able to achieve your goal. Everything takes time and hard work.

B.Y.O.B.:   What's the typical cost of a personal trainer?

Amanda: Costs of a trainer can range from thirty dollars to hundreds of dollars for a session or multiple sessions. Depends on the club you are in, or if you hire a personal trainer to come to your house.

B.Y.O.B.:   What are the benefits with working with a trainer?

Amanda: There are many benefits when working with a trainer.

1. Motivation
2. Improving your overall fitness
3. Change up the same old boring workouts that you've been doing
4. More of a challenge
5. You want to see results
6. You need a *push*!

B.Y.O.B.:   What is your opinion about dieting?

Amanda: My view on dieting is to eat healthy and stay healthy. Have a "cheat" day but don't go overboard. You can have ice cream but don't eat the entire container.

B.Y.O.B.:   I do not believe in those fad diets that celebrities are doing. Okay, they can work but the odds are that the weight you lost will come back once you are off the diet and you are more likely to add a few more pounds back on also.

B.Y.O.B.:   Usually how long does it take to see improvement?

Amanda: Depends on the person and how committed they are. Usually you will see a change within weeks. Most of my clients see change in three to six weeks. I tell my clients I do my part of the job, now when you leave you have to do your part by eating healthy and staying healthy. You will see the results you are looking for.

B.Y.O.B.:   What will be your advice for young women to stay healthy?

Amanda: Eat breakfast! Think of your body like a car, if there is no gas in your tank you are going to get nowhere. You need to be constantly fueling your body. Your body needs food and nutrients—this is your energy and the fuel to get you through the day.

B.Y.O.B.: In your opinion, why do people give up? It's like they start so strong, and then stop.

Amanda: I have seen this one too many times. I can't tell you how many men and women say, "I was so good last month, then I just gave up." I tell them they have to stay committed! You can't see change overnight! I would be nice about it, but I would let them know there is a reason why they got to be that way. It may have taken months or years to put on that weight. Well, it's going to take you months or years to get that weight off. It's about the inches—how do your clothes fit now? Don't worry about it if the weight isn't coming off quick enough.

B.Y.O.B.: From your personal experience in seeing someone who has accomplished their weight goal, how does their confidence change?

Amanda: For sure I see their body, personality, and confidence change. I hear a lot of things, and sometimes a little TMI. But you build this relationship with them and you become so close that really nothing is surprising anymore. I hear "I got my sexy back" or "my spouse looks at me and loves me more and my *body*." I'm glad I can be there to give them support and encourage them to do better. I tell them I do my part here in the gym, once you go through the gym doors you are accountable for what happens out there.

B.Y.O.B.: What are some tools to use online to help track your weight loss and food intake?

Amanda: I use My Net Diary. I have it on my iPhone; it's super easy to work and it's a great tool to calculate what you have eaten that day, your workouts, and water intake. It also tells you how many calories you need that day to reach your goal weight. You can also use My Fitness Pal as well.

B.Y.O.B.: To you when you hear Be Your Own Beautiful, what does that mean to you?

Amanda: To be confident in your own skin! Don't stress to be like your favorite celebrity—they get paid to look the way they do. They have private chefs and train constantly. In the real world that just isn't logical.

B.Y.O.B.: I love that, Amanda! Thank you so much for your honesty in this interview!

Amanda: Sure, no problem. Anything else you need, just let me know!

B.Y.O.B.: Thank you so much!

Interview with:

Rikki Burke

> "Book your next appointment and become glamorous; see for yourself what the FUSS is all about . . ."

Interview with Rikki Burke

(HAIRSYLIST)

Rikki S. Burke was born on April 22, 1979, in Dallas, Texas, talented and gifted from birth. At the age of thirteen, she began to do family and friends' hair, but her love and desire came at the age of fifteen. Immediately she knew her talent for making ladies look and feel glamorous about themselves was a gift from God.

Rikki had a desire to make it happen. Rikki completed her education at ITC Academy, and she continues her education in her field of making women look and feel great about being beautiful, being the entrepreneur she is.

Rikki is motivated by God and two very special men in her life—her sons, Trayton and Bryce Turner—as well as family and great friends, and she continues to make sure all who enter the doors of *Rikki Burke Salons* will leave glamorous.

B.Y.O.B.:   Rikki, I just want to say thank you for being a part of this project (Be Your Own Beautiful) and let you know that I chose you to be a part of this because I believe you do very good work. When I came into your shop there was not a lot of gossip and you have a wonderful personality.

Rikki: Thank you! Thank you for choosing me.

B.Y.O.B.:   For my readers who don't know who Rikki is, tell us about yourself.

Rikki: I'm a master stylist, a mother, and a hard worker.

B.Y.O.B.:   What is your background? When did you start doing hair?

Rikki: I started doing hair really young. I started when I was thirteen or fourteen and I started doing hair in our apartment, charging ten or fifteen dollars here and there. I tell everybody that this (doing hair) is a gift from God. My mother used to have *Ebony* and *Essence* magazines. I would open up the books and go from there. I was able to do exactly what you asked me to do if it was in the book.

B.Y.O.B.:   So being a hair stylist, was this always a dream of yours?

Rikki: It's just dropped in my life—it's like God just said "Here, this is yours." It was just something to do. My family has always been in fashion and styling in one way or another, so this pretty much dropped in my lap. It wasn't a dream, it wasn't a vision, it was just a "go."

B.Y.O.B.: And you love to do hair?

Rikki: I love to do hair!

B.Y.O.B.: What is your signature look?

Rikki: My signature look is soft and flowing—healthy hair with curls.

B.Y.O.B.: Do you wear a lot of sew-ins or weaves?

Rikki: It's a system that I do. Basically, I will wear my own hair (just relaxed or permed). I will wear it for about two months before I go to put my weaves in.

B.Y.O.B.: So you just did my hair not too long ago, and this Texas weather is so humid. What is your advice to me or anyone that is reading this book on how to take care of your weave in the heat?

Rikki: Well, first of all you have to be a soldier to even wear a weave in this heat (we share a laugh.) especially if it's long. But I would say keep the maintenance up on it. Keep it washed! But if you wear your own hair make sure you keep a heat protector on it. Make sure when you wash it, you wash it in cool water, not hot water, and use a leave-in conditioner. And keep less heat on your hair like flat-ironing it and curling it.

B.Y.O.B.: You said a heat protector—what is that?

Rikki: It comes in an oil base or a spray. So if you had to use a flatiron or blow-dryer, it is a coat to protect your hair because heat can cause split ends and damage.

Devin Brown

B.Y.O.B.: What is your favorite type of hair to work on?

Rikki: My favorite type of hair to work on . . . I love to work on all types of hair. On the natural side, it's more complicated because you are dealing with all kinds of textures of hair, especially those who are transitioning to natural—you've got to get in and train it. It gets easier as the clients keep coming in every two weeks. But when they first start, it can be more coarse and brittle. I have a couple of natural clients and once we shampoo and blow-dry it, it's manageable. I love what I do and I have my dedicated clients, but I am trying to come back from behind the chair all day, go more behind the scenes. I want to tap more into makeup and training.

B.Y.O.B.: So maybe like opening up your own beauty school or something?

Rikki: No, I don't want to take it that far. (We share a laugh.) But I will probably do classes like advanced classes for stylists; my school that I graduated from asked me to come back and be an instructor, but I don't think I have the patience.

B.Y.O.B.: It's a lot to teach someone how to do something.

Rikki: Yes, and it's different individuals; you have some that are like me, that have the eye and the gift, then there's the one that just wants to learn. With me I am more of a visual person—you can show me something and I got it. So you do have to have patience to teach everybody on any level.

B.Y.O.B.: I agree about people born with the gift. You can tell people that were born with the gift versus the ones that just learned the skill. You can definitely tell the difference.

Rikki: You would be amazed at how many of the girls didn't know how to hold a curling iron.

B.Y.O.B.: Wow! Well, with that being said, what would you say is your biggest challenge?

Rikki: My biggest challenge would be coloring hair: mixing the color, customizing a color. Not actually applying it, that's not a big deal for me. But the chemistry of it—that probably is the only thing I would have to sit and give some thought to.

B.Y.O.B.: Now is coloring and bleaching your hair damaging?

Rikki: It can be! Especially with African Americans—I don't think we should double up. You got where you want to relax your hair, and then you want to color your hair for the exquisiteness of it—that's doing too much. It needs to be one or the other every six to eight weeks. Some beauticians do overlap, but I don't!

B.Y.O.B.: So how would you say hair relates to one's personal style?

Rikki: Your hair shows you, your lifestyle, your appearance. You have some that wear Mohawks—I would say she is more risky and a little bit edgy. You have those who are conservative, laid-back—they usually wear a soft look. So your hair really does say a lot about you.

B.Y.O.B.: Have you ever had someone to come into your shop and their self-esteem is low, but by the time they leave, their confidence is up?

Rikki: Yes, I have had women come in and when they sat in the chair they slumped, not very sociable. And this is what I love about my job—they come in one way, but they leave looking and feeling another, and to be able to give people that type of feeling makes me feel good. You don't have to have clothes, but if you get your hair done, you feel like you look good. On the other hand, you can have on the cutest outfit and if your hair isn't done, you're just not feeling it. So your hair says a lot!

Devin Brown

B.Y.O.B.:   That is the truth!

B.Y.O.B.:   I know that you kind of touched on this a little bit, but what is your dream goal?

Rikki: I would like to open a chain of Rikki Burke salons around the world. I'd also like to be able to tap into makeup. I am a point where I want to learn more—doing hair has become second nature to me. I want to go behind the scenes.

B.Y.O.B.:   Who inspires you? Where do you get your motivation from?

Rikki: Who inspires me? God and my children—they motivate me. I have a thing where I am never comfortable so I strive, strive, strive! I know that there is somewhere else I am supposed to be and I am just reaching for it. But when I look at my clients, a lot of them have been with me for ten and fifteen years, and they are still coming and they come to me and feel like I can do everything in the world. I had a client that came to me and said, "Rikki, you know your name is out there, but your spirit is so humble." I am amazed when people come in the shop and tell me someone referred them to me. I just don't see it like others see it. I just get up and do my job and my mind is on constant overdrive, trying to see a better way to succeed, and that's basically it. I'm not caught up in the hype or the fame—I'm really not! That's what keeps me going.

B.Y.O.B.:   I will have to agree about you being humble. When I came to you, I liked how there wasn't any drama or gossip in the atmosphere of your shop, because I, too, am a very laid-back person.

Rikki: I get that a lot. I actually had someone recently tell me how they like the atmosphere in my shop. Concerning my clients, that is one of my main goals—to not make my salon a typical beauty shop. We, as women, have a lot to deal with: kids, job, etc., so coming here, let's make it where you can relax and have nice conversation and good music. I never believe in the "beauty shop"—I think that's why I have always had my own salon.

B.Y.O.B.: Earlier when we were talking about your dream assignment, you were saying you would like to have your shops everywhere. Have you traveled?

Rikki: Oh, yeah. That's why they call me the international master stylist. (We share a laugh.) I put together some things on my own, as well. For instance, I have been to Italy. Right after Katrina I went to New Orleans every other weekend to do hair there and help out. I have been to Atlanta. I have certain clients whose homes I will travel to for an extra fee. Also, I go to nursing homes. I believe in giving back. I haven't had a chance to travel lately, though, not since I had my children.

B.Y.O.B.: Tell us about your non-profit organization.

Rikki: I am a dreamer and I set goals. Once I set my mind to something, I do my best to try to make it happen. I went to school at the age of nineteen, from there I worked under someone. I opened up my first salon at the age of twenty-two. I have always wanted my own place—this is my third salon. The Doll Squad, a non-profit organization, was started by me and a friend of mine. It's an empowerment group for young ladies, teaching them how to be women and how to go for what they want in life, and how to be leaders. My friend and I were sitting at my kitchen table when that came about. We started brainstorming and talking it out and that was it. It was August of 2012 and by December, that's when we did the Players' Ball.

We wanted to come up with something that we could give back. I came from "the hood" and you see a lot, and there are a lot of children that don't have anything. Where I came from, you could sit on your front porch and see boys sagging and young girls talking about nothing, but that is our next generation. And it's our responsibility to help where we can, even if it's saying something positive or motivating to that child.

B.Y.O.B.: I always say inspire others by being you, because if they can take your words and use them to inspire the next person, then it becomes a domino effect. It's hard for me to get up right now in front of a group (We share a laugh.), but I love to inspire people—it gives me so much joy just to see other people doing well in their own life, and I react as if it were me.

Rikki: Yes! You have people, who sit back and point a finger, but what are you going to do about it? And that's how I am, especially with the youth. The Doll Squad I really love—I will cry in a minute when I look at those girls, and it's a beautiful thing when they can leave and feel like they have received something positive. And those hugs and to hear I love you; it means something because we don't have to know one another to love one another.

B.Y.O.B.: When I spoke at the Doll Squad, I freaked out, but just in that little bit of time I really learned something. When I got up there, I started so strong but just the look on their faces—it didn't look as though they were paying attention. I was intimidated by the girls. Later, when the girls were asked which of the three speakers they remembered most, every last girl who was called on referred to something I had said. I wasn't even up there a good five minutes because I freaked out, so when I was about to leave and had quite a few girls come up to me and hug me, it said a lot. So now I know not to be intimidated when you think no one is paying attention—I just keep on and "do me."

Rikki: Yes! Do you! You have to go with the flow and you will become more relaxed. I ask God all the time to speak through me, give something to give these "babies," and He never fails.

Devin Brown

B.Y.O.B.: He is so faithful.

Rikki: Right now Doll Squad is focused on girls, but we are working on bringing something in for the young men, because it's important for them to know how to love and be loved, and let them know it's okay for them to cry and you don't have to be so hard.

B.Y.O.B.: That is so true. Even with *Be Your Own Beautiful,* I have had men come up to me and say, "You know, we men need to hear that too." And that just blows me away.

Rikki: That is true—we can't leave our young men out! We, as a whole, have to know that God can bring us through anything, and we don't have to be caught up in the system. I have been through a lot in my life, and I tell the young people that I work with them not because of what I have heard, but because of what I have been through. And I tell you this so you don't have to bump your head so hard, because you're going to bump it, but it doesn't have to be so difficult.

B.Y.O.B.: That is true. I always use this analogy. Life is like a battery. In order for the battery to work, it has negative and it has positive, and you need both for it to work. In life, it might be hard to see the positive in a negative situation. It might be small, but draw from it, and I promise you if you pray and focus on the positive and not so much on the negative, it's going to be all right. Before you know it, that problem is over—you're going to turn around and say, "I did it, I came from that. How did I get from there to here?"

Rikki: That's good!

B.Y.O.B.: You know, even with going back to me speaking at the Doll Squad, I also was inspired my sister, Sharae Brown. She called me—and I still get teary-eyed when I think about it—but she called after me I presented. "Devin, every time I

Devin Brown

think about you speaking that day, I get teary-eyed. You have come so far. You used to be so mean and judgmental that I couldn't be around, couldn't stand you, but to see where you are now—you inspire me." But the truth is she inspired me first, when she told me I'm not Mama, that I am a big sister. It made me look at myself and ask, "Well, who is Devin? Because if I'm not Mama, then who am I?" But they have inspired me, and now I just want to share it. People think "Oh my mother wasn't on drugs or out selling herself" and think they don't have a story, but they do!

Rikki: That is a beautiful thing when your sister can see your growth.

B.Y.O.B.: Since we are talking about growth . . . Have you ever had a desire to work with celebrity clients?

Rikki: That is a goal of mine, but what I am excited about is I have someone coming to show me about makeup, and I want to be able to expand my horizons that way. I want to get into something that gets me out of my comfort zone.

B.Y.O.B.: That is true. I said earlier on in my book that in order to reach your destiny you have to come out of your comfort zone.

B.Y.O.B.: What are your three favorite styling products and why?

Rikki: I really like the Influence line. The relaxer is really good and they have awesome conditioners. I also like Bed Head.

B.Y.O.B.: Okay! So what are some of the biggest mistakes you see people make with their hair?

Rikki: The biggest mistake is putting too much heat on their hair. Some more no-nos are women who try to dye their own hair, over-processed hair, and when wearing a quick weave the way they are gluing the hair directly on top of their own hair and it brings your hair out.

B.Y.O.B.:   So what are some good tips on managing your hair when wearing weave or braids?

Rikki: With wigs, I will say don't wear them every day—allow your hair to breathe. Wearing a wig constantly is like smothering your hair. With sew-in weaves, your scalp can still breathe if you get your maintenance every two to three weeks. I am not a big fan of grease because it clogs your pores; my main thing is to keep your hair conditioned. Braids are good because your scalp is breathing as long as whoever is braiding it does not start off the braid with a lot of tension and cause you to lose your edges. But I'm not big on braids; I really only braid for my sew-ins.

B.Y.O.B.:   What do you believe makes a good stylist?

Rikki: Their personality and their craft.

B.Y.O.B.:   I like that and I have to agree with that!

B.Y.O.B.:   If I were to ask you what does "*Be Your Own Beautiful*" mean . . . what would your response be?

Rikki: Be Your Own Beautiful—that is a powerful statement within itself. Be your own beautiful no matter what your color is, how nappy your hair is, how straight it is. Love you, and know who you are. And remember you have nothing to prove to anyone but God and yourself. Treat people positive; treat them the way you want to be treated. That's being your own beautiful inside and out. I always tell my girls just because you're cute on the outside doesn't mean that you're beautiful on the inside—you have to watch what comes out of your mouth. You don't have to be in the in-crowd—you stand out and be you and love yourself, that way you can love everybody else. Don't let people tear you down. So be your own beautiful—that's a good one. That is an awesome title because it says a lot within itself. It doesn't matter how old you are when that light goes off and you get it.

B.Y.O.B.: You know when you said don't let anyone tear you down. That is so true—you are not supposed to let anyone define who you are. Those types of relationships are so unhealthy.

Rikki: Absolutely! I had a young girl sit in my seat and she was saying that some girls at her school were saying that she was big, and I told her the next time they say that, tell them, "Okay. I looked in the mirror (We share a laugh.) and what, if you're going to love me, love me for me." Now if it's something regarding someone's heath, then find a nice way to say something, and say it out of love.

B.Y.O.B.: That is so true! I like that "okay, I looked in the mirror"—that's cute! I tell my friends all the time, "If you have something to say to me, please do, but do it out of love because I want to be able to receive it."

Rikki: Exactly.

B.Y.O.B.: I just want to say to you, Rikki, thank you so much for being a part of *Be Your Own Beautiful*.

Rikki: You are welcome, and thank you! I hope that I answered all your questions, because I was nervous with this being my first interview.

B.Y.O.B.: Yes! You were great!

Rikki: I appreciate being chosen, seriously.

B.Y.O.B.: You are so welcome. Thank you again!

To reach Rikki you can go to:

Her establishment:

11418 Audelia Rd.
Dallas, TX 75243
Phone: (888) 224-2865

Online:

www.rikkiburke.com
www.styleseat.com/rikkiburke.com

Facebook: Rikki Burke

Twitter: @Rikkiburke

INTERVIEW WITH:

Cherise Riley

> "Helping others to pursue their purpose so they can embrace their destiny."

How important are you're . . .

GOALS, VISION BOARD, DREAMS, & INSPIRATIONS

Who is Cherise L. Riley?

Born on May 3, 1974, in the beautiful city of Hollywood, Florida.

- Inspirational and motivational speaker
- Author, entrepreneur, life coach, and mentor
- Licensed and ordained as a Minister of the Gospel
- Founder of Destiny Empowerment International
- Founder of Sons & Daughters of Destiny Outreach Ministries

- Founder of The Project PAD (Purpose and Destiny) Academy
- Television & radio personality of Destiny Empowerment Hour

The LIFE:

Well, it could be said that she and her story are one in the same! Cherise Riley is a young woman who has overcome life's obstacles and has defied the odds by beating death. Cherise has endured abandonment, molestation, rape, and abuse—emotional, verbal, mental, and physical. She has also dealt with low self-esteem, rejection, church hurt, depression, and homelessness. Wanting the hurt and pain to end, not understanding why she wasn't loved or wanted, Cherise did the only thing her empty heart could identify with—she turned to death.

She attempted to end her life on three separate occasions. After this period of turmoil, Cherise began to question God as to why he wanted her to live. What was His purpose for her life and why was she having to go through all of this torment to get there?

God simply answered, "For much is given, much is required. My son had to endure it, so why not you?"

The little girl who had endured such harsh things in her life, though she had become a woman, was still trapped and lost. Cherise was tied to the past and too afraid to come out of the dark for fear of having to tell her story. But God was able to resurrect her and gave her a new life. She learned forgiveness and the true meaning of *agape* love. She became a vessel to be used by God to help the countless others throughout the world get their breakthrough as well.

Cherise's belief and focus is for an international platform to motivate people, enabling them to conquer fears, learn forgiveness, understand the power of love, and learn how to reactivate Faith in order to pursue purpose and embrace destiny. She has a message that affects people from every walk of life, background, gender, age, and nationality. The vision God has placed in her heart is global and designed to reach the world!

"But what about you," He asked. "Who do you say I am?"—Matthew 16:15

The view we have of ourselves most of the time can be one-dimensional. I asked a group of young adults I was mentoring a few years back to name a few attributes that they believed described themselves the most. I then was bold enough to ask them to share a few about me . . . and after a few sarcastic attempts using words like quiet, unpredictable, and reserved, I jokingly asked "Do you really *know* who I am?"

In Matthew 16, Jesus wanted to know what everyone else saw in Him and if His disciples were able to recognize His true distinctiveness. The general crowd knew that Jesus was a man of God, but only Peter recognized Him as the Son of God. Jesus didn't ask for validation or affirmation of His identity, because He already knew who He was and what He was called to accomplish. Too many times *we* are looking for others to stroke us, sugar-coat us, and affirm us, but if you aren't able to recognize yourself, how can anyone else recognize you? We're often told not to care about the thoughts of others, but as Kingdom citizens, we *must* know if our lives are accurately reflecting the lifestyle we *say* we represent. Do people know who you really are?

What do men say about you? That can be like opening a can of worms for some folks or a refreshing review for others. Ask yourself, has your personal credibility recovered? Are people happy to see you coming? Or glad to see you *leave*? Do they believe you are sincere or do they think you are fake? Do you think you are kind when others know you as rude? Friends, let your talk and your walk be aligned and in one accord because we are living in a three-dimensional, two-way-mirrored world. Not only are we considerate of how God sees us and how we view ourselves, we must *also* be mindful that we are living apostles to the world, especially when we say we represent Christ. People are watching everything about us, not just what we say, but also our *actions*! Knowing who you are should be comparable with knowing who Jesus is and by the way we conduct our lives, Jesus can justifiably ask us the same question . . . When our speech and walk doesn't line up, it contradicts itself. So when Jesus looks upon us he should see *Himself*, and when he doesn't you just may be asked, "Do you know who I *am*?" Let's make

Devin Brown

sure that no matter who looks upon us or what view they see that they always see Christ in us not just in our talk but also in our daily walk!

HOW DO WE REACH OUR DREAMS?

B.Y.O.B.: **I believe we do this by being proactive.**

Creating a new vision for our future based on success, happiness, and well-being.

I believe in order to manifest your desires, it requires you to clearly articulate what it is you want to achieve.

B.Y.O.B.: I wanted to do this part with you in my book because you have watered the seed in my life when it came to me and helped me reach and push for my goals. I'm still learning, but you have been right by my side, coaching me along the way. You have not only been a friend and like a sister to me, but also my mentor. You don't have the "crab syndrome"—you taught me that—and I can appreciate that. You have truly been someone that adds to my life, and I know that you are God-sent to me and I love you for just that alone. And I wanted my B.Y.O.B. readers to have some type of foundation to start their dreams and to get them thinking in life, so if I'm the one sowing or watering when they read this book, I want them to grasp it and begin to reach for their destiny, because I truly believe everyone has a purpose here on Earth.

Cherise Riley: You are absolutely correct, Devin. Everyone has been given a purpose on this Earth and when we discover that purpose we are then able to truly begin to embrace our destiny. I'm honored that you would consider me as a mentor to you, because I only see myself as a person who has been through a lot in life, and from the hard knocks and many lessons that have been learned, I only truly desire to be used in such a way as to help others not make the same mistakes, and to also not allow their past—hurts, disappointments, heartbreaks, broken homes, low self-esteem, molestation, etc.—to determine their future! We truly reach our dreams when we stop living in our past and stop allowing others to keep us in the past as well. You stated in the beginning that people need to create a new vision for their future and that vision should be based on success, happiness, and well-being. I also believe that vision needs to be first and foremost based on God's perfect will for our lives because when we have a person who has been through what seems to be a living hell, it's hard to paint a picture of anything positive because all they see is the negative. So it's important that we learn to seek out God's will and purpose for us so that we can understand the past, learn from it, embrace it, and move on from it to be *able* to create something new. Because a lot of times we have plans for ourselves and they don't line up with God's plans, because our vision for ourselves is too small, and we need to begin to think outside the box and reach higher.

B.Y.O.B.: I believe goal setting requires S.M.A.R.T. goals. Can you elaborate on this?

Cherise Riley: In order to obtain a goal you have to have direction on how to get there. What I mean by that is this: say you want to take a trip to London. The goal is getting to London; however, there are some steps that need to be taken before you can reach the desired ending point. There has to be a timeframe in mind; you also have to consider the cost, mode of transportation of getting there, who is going with you, and what you plan on doing once you have reached your desired destination. So when we equate this to setting personal goals for our lives as it pertains to pursuing purpose and reaching destiny, we have to take on the same mindset. Once you know what it is you are supposed to be doing . . . Then you are correct, Devin, you have to be S.M.A.R.T.

S—SPECIFIC: Be certain as to what it is you are trying to achieve. You can't waiver in this area; there has to be certainty and assurance.

M—MEASURABLE: You have to be able to estimate what is to be expected and have planned steps to reach your desired ending.

A—ACHIEVABLE: You have to set goals that are truly attainable and able to be carried out successfully.

R—REALISTIC: This one is kind of touchy to me, because I don't believe in dealing with reality based on "*this world*" system, because if my current situation is bleak and dim then being realistic according to this world says that there is no way I can ever be better than I currently am. However, when I walk in *faith* and become realistic according to what God has said about me and my situation, then I can carry it through and overcome any and every obstacle of the past, present, and future to obtain my goal. Being realistic to me means not going *ahead* of God, but going *with* God concerning the visions, dreams, and goals given to me, because when I go *with* him instead of *in front* of him, I'm then assured to reach and obtain them.

T—TIME FRAMES: Setting time frames for yourself is very important. However, being wise in setting these time frames is just as necessary. If one of your goals, dreams, or desires is to leave your job and be your own boss, then you have to take all the necessary steps to make that happen. You have to begin to plan and set small target dates to reach that goal or destination. If you know it will take thirty thousand dollars to start your own business and you only have five hundred saved, then you would need to set up target dates as to when you will reach your goal and what you plan on doing to hit it.

B.Y.O.B.:   What is one characteristic that you believe every leader should possess?

Cherise Riley: The number one characteristic, hands down, that I feel every leader should possess is *humility*! Because real leaders are selfless, and they live to help others! It's never about them or their gain, but rather about how it will impact or affect other's lives.

B.Y.O.B.:   What is the primary thing needed to build an appropriate and rewarding career?

Cherise Riley: Education! What I mean by that is educating yourself in the field that you desire to conquer. You want to write a book, and then do your research on what it takes to do so from publishing to advertising to publicity coverage, etc. You want to be a personal trainer, then there are things you will need to know first before becoming one. The Bible says that people perish for lack of knowledge and this is so very true. If we spent half the time reading and researching and educating ourselves on the things that we desired to do as we spent on watching reality TV then we would always be on top of our game. But sadly, we are living in a day and time that reality TV, which is not so realistic, has become more of a priority to us than bettering our personal lives. Then we wonder why we are still stuck in the same old dead-end job, barely making enough to cover our bills, and then we want to pray and ask God to bless us, when He has already done and given us everything we need to become successful on this Earth. But *we* have to be willing to take the necessary steps and stop being lazy to achieve it.

B.Y.O.B.: Besides reading B.Y.O.B. (laughing), what do you suggest people read to give them a good prospective on their dreams?

Cherise Riley: Well, one of my all-time favorite books is by Napoleon Hill. *Think and Grow Rich*—this is not just talking about financial wealth, but becoming rich emotionally, spiritually, and mentally, as well. Also another favorite by him is *The Law of Success*, and of course I believe everyone should research and find books and articles pertaining to the field or industry they are trying to tap into. The only way to be successful in an area goes back to what I stated earlier, and that's through educating yourself in that area. Instead of spending all day on Facebook and Twitter, how about going to Google and searching out the field you want to go in and reading up on it, search out people who are already successful in that area and read about how they accomplished their goals. I believe that we don't always have to reinvent the wheel, we can learn from others. Now, there may be things you encounter that others did not and that is fine, but for the most part—trust me, someone else has already gone through what you are and will be able to help you through it.

B.Y.O.B.: What barriers could block the way for many? And what can be done about it?

Cherise Riley: Wow. So many things come to mind with this question. But the main and most common barriers are fear, people, and our past. Fear is the most common of them all though, because most people don't just fear failing, but they fear success, too. That may sound strange, but because the higher up you go, the longer the fall, it can cause trepidation. For instance, if you only stand on the curb and you fall (fail), it's easy to get up from that and more than likely there will be no real injuries sustained. However, if you are at the top of an eighty-story building and you fall (fail), more than likely you will sustain life-altering injuries. And fear causes people to avoid success, because they focus on what could happen if they fail once they reach the top. But we have to learn how to change that fear into faith. Trust and believe that God will never take us to a place if he isn't able to keep us there.

Also, what ties into this is people! We oftentimes attach the wrong people to our lives, visions, businesses, dreams, and desires because they are our family or childhood friend, etc. And when those people don't understand our vision or dreams, or when their faith is lacking, they have a way of planting negative seeds into your spirit that will cause you to begin to waver. So you have to begin to watch *who* you share your vision with, especially in the building stages, because just like a house, when the foundation is being poured it's very important that no foreign object is on the ground because it has the ability to offset the foundation and over time, it can and will cause a crack and break in the foundation. When your foundation is not solid and firm, everything that is built upon it will not stand properly, either.

The last thing that is most common is our past. We allow our past mistakes to hinder us; we focus on the negativity of our past instead of allowing our past to be a building block that launches us into a much more prosperous and blessed future. Our past teaches us lessons of what not to do and we should learn from those things instead of allowing those things to stop us from moving past it.

B.Y.O.B.: What do you want to achieve in your career and why?

Cherise Riley: I desire to accomplish every dream, vision, goal, and purpose that has been birthed inside of me. I want to be used by God to help birth out as many men and women in this world as possible, helping them to break free from their past to embrace the beauty and brightness of their future. I desire to leave a legacy that protects and impacts the future generations of our world. I desire to see people set free and live the life God ordained for them to live and this is important to me because God did it for me! He brought me through so much and I believe that he did it because it was and is my purpose in life to help many others. It's my burning desire to make sure I don't leave this earth until I have fulfilled that, whether it's through writing books, mentoring programs, radio and television broadcasts, or whatever avenue is made available to me. I want to help people be successful because that is the one thing that truly brings me fulfillment in my life.

B.Y.O.B.:   What do you think our readers can gain by spending time by themselves and increasing their talent or increasing their character to help toward their dream?

Cherise Riley: I believe that spending time with oneself gives you the opportunity to learn who *you* really are! Being left alone with your own thoughts and ideas gives you the time to filter out the opinions and voices of all the others around you and be able to hear clearly your own voice and desires as well as God's voice and desires for your life. I'm not saying that we shouldn't have friends or be around people, but what I am saying is that you need to have a balance and shouldn't be afraid to be by yourself sometimes, because it's actually healthy. Find out who you are, what you like, what makes you happy, because most of the time we find when we are always around others we tend to take on their likes and interests instead of finding our own and when they are not around we tend to be lost. So when you spend time alone with your own thoughts you are more likely to find what it is that actually drives you! What you like, what makes you happy, etc., and these are key points of discovery that will assist in character building and being successful in your goals.

B.Y.O.B.: How can a person strengthen their foundation of personal credibility?

Cherise Riley: The only way to strengthen your foundation when it comes to credibility is by walking in integrity. Being a person of your word, being willing to help others and give back. People don't respect selfish people, so when we are cognizant of that then we have the ability to build our credibility even more. Credibility is the key when trying to sell a product or offer a service. If people trust you as a person, then they are more than likely to trust what you are offering, as well.

B.Y.O.B.: How can a person arrange their days so they can become unstoppable?

Cherise Riley: This goes back to what we stated in the beginning—being S.M.A.R.T. You have to dedicate a certain portion of your day to your purpose (visions, goals, dreams, etc.). Just like we set our DVR to record shows we don't want to miss, we have to set aside time in our lives on a daily bases to work on our vision. I personally in my own life try to dedicate the same amount of time to my personal ventures as I do to my current job. It's called small sacrifices, and I say small because it can never be compared to the amazing benefits you obtain when you completely reach that desired place you are aiming toward. If I invest eight hours a day helping to build someone else's vision, then I need to be willing to invest as much or at least half of the same time to my own vision. If that means cutting the TV off, then so be it, because at the end of the day *Love and Hip Hop, Mary Mary, Vince and Tamar, The Braxtons,* or whatever else is on TV is *not* going help me reach my vision, purpose, or destiny! So instead of investing the time making them richer by tuning in to the shows all the time, you need to change up your priorities and focus on the vision, purpose, and goals you have set for yourself. Now I'm not saying to stop supporting those shows, but what I am saying is you need to have balance in order to be successful. You can't spend eight hours a day at work, come home and spend five to six hours in front of the television, and then spend ten minutes working toward your vision and expect to be successful. That's just not going to happen.

B.Y.O.B.:   How can a person leave their mark wherever they go?

Cherise Riley: This goes back to character and integrity. I always say a title only tells me what you are skilled to do—Author, CEO, Actor, etc.—but your *character* tells me who you really are! We leave a mark everywhere we go; the question is how do we leave a positive mark? And that answer is based on character. Because what's in you is what will come out of you. If you are selfish, rude, disrespectful, and mean, then that's what people are going to remember about you. But if you are kind, humble, knowledgeable, helpful, respectful, honest, and have integrity, then that's what people will remember. So your attitude will always determine your altitude in life.

B.Y.O.B.:   When you hear Be Your Own Beautiful, what does that mean to you?

Cherise Riley: It means be the person God designed me to be from the inside out. Be a person of integrity, be a person who leads by example, be the kind of person who has their own identity and who is comfortable and confident in whom God created them to be. Loving every part of me, even the past because without it I would not be the person who I am today, I would not have the strength I have or the passion. Being my own beautiful is being the kind of person I would like to see on this Earth decades from now, leaving such a legacy that others would follow.

Cherise can be contacted at:

www.DestinyEmpowerment.com
www.twitter.com/DEPROJECT
www.blogtalkradio.com/DestinyEmpowermentproject

Rare Beauties

I hope and pray that everything that I have said in this book has helped each and every one of you. I pray that this has begun something new in you, something you can share with others. If you need to go back and reread this or take several chapters at a time and concentrate on them and live them until you get it right, that's okay.

I believe in this journey of finding you, you will realize what a beautiful jewel you are, and the things you deserve, that you don't have to settle for anything or anyone. Remember to inspire others by just simply being you.

Remember to be a good friend, a good sister, a good daughter, and a good *you*! Remember when I did the breakdown of God, communication, and friendship—use that in all the relationships that you have. Don't carry around the word "friend" too lightly—not everyone can hold up to the potential of being what you need in them as a friend, not everyone has found themselves. You still can love them and go on, you can share this book with them to help them get to where you are; just don't let them bring you down.

I wanted to also give you another nugget and that is: it's okay to have role models, but don't idolize anyone—be your own true self. I myself have different people I look up to for certain things, but I never make them my idol.

Idol means an image used as an object of worship, a false god, one that is adored, often blindly or excessively, or something visible but without substance.

Or

<u>Idolize:</u> To regard with blind admiration or devotion, to worship as an idol.

God is the only one we should worship.

With that being said, I don't mind being your mentor, big sister, or just simply someone you look up to.

Also, don't forget about your goals in life, your dreams, and your visions. They can be done if you push toward them. Don't let anyone tell you they can't, because *they can*! *You can*!

Your choices today can affect your tomorrow. Choose wisely, stay positive, and keep God first.

I also want my RARE BEAUTIES to know that a woman can wear nothing more beautiful than her confidence!

And remember, this will not happen overnight; however, as soon as you take your first step, the closer you will become to being *you*!

Here's my information, this is set up for all my Rare Beauties and I will try to respond to as many as I can.

Email: <u>byob.everything@gmail.com</u>

Blog: follow my posthttp://beutifullyrare.blogspot.com

FACEBOOK: Devin Be Your Own Beautiful Brown

Website: <u>www.everythingdevin.com</u>

I love you all.

This page is dedicated to Isaac Smith.

I went to church with him and every Sunday he would, after singing on the praise team, come down and ask me for my autograph after church. For the longest time I never knew or understood why he did that! But he would always make me smile, and in reply I would always say, "I got you!" Well on May 20, 2012, Isaac passed. Not too long ago I realized that he was speaking something into my life, and I wanted to keep my word to him, and let him be the first to get an autographed copy of my book. He still won in the end since I didn't ever give him that "one" autograph, he got plenty.

To Isaac: thank you so much for seeing past way more than I could imagine within myself at the time, and even though you would jokingly say it, I knew you were serious. Sometimes I can still hear your voice and see those deep dimples when you'd say, "I'm going to need your autograph after church." Well, as I promised, Isaac—I GOT YOU!

I will never forget that you probably unknowingly encouraged me.

Forever Grateful,

Devin Brown

Dedication

I dedicate this book to my loving grandmother, my best friend, Mary D. Jackson.

Her words to me on a birthday card the year she passed:

> *Dear Devin,*
>
> *I can't ask for a better granddaughter than you. You have made me very proud; you are now entering into the other phase of your life, becoming a lady. And I hope that you make me just as proud by taking it slow, taking God with you every step of the way. I pray that God keep you covered under the Blood and protect you from the wilds of the devil that is just waiting for an innocent soul like yours.*
>
> *Love always,*
> *Granny*

Granny, I hope I have done just that . . . made you proud of me! I love you so much and your memory will never be forgotten.

And . . .

To my mother, Karen Brown: I love you, my dear, you are doing so well, and I love that our relationship has beat the odds. You have supported me in writing this book to help inspire others, and I'm so grateful for that—this has made us much closer. I know that if you keep on this journey of finding who you are, you will see that exceptional beauty of that butterfly that I saw a while ago. I hope that I have shown you that we can move on from the past and succeed at what God has planned for us and you. I love you, Mommy . . .

And finally to my sisters Raetequa Brown and Aundrea Brown: You guys were the first to inspire me and have motivated me to look deep within myself and find that inner beauty . . . and now I have the courage to inspire others to do the same! I love you both so much. Oh, yeah—y'all still my babies.

Acknowledgements

Special Thanks (This will be a little long, but hey—cut me a break, this is my first book.)

To God: I have realized through this whole process that You are my Connect, and all You're doing is connecting me with other people. I am so grateful to be called Your friend and Your child. I am grateful for the gift of writing. I'm thankful to know the real You, and not get caught up in religion. And I have been blessed to know who I am in You. I'm loving it, I'm loving me and who I have become in You. And most of all I love You.

I want to also give special thanks to Cherise Riley, my friend and my sister, for your support, your wisdom, and for being a woman that likes to see other women succeed. You don't have the crab syndrome (pulling others down to get to the top). Love you dearly, my friend.

Also to my Pastor, Pastor Porter L. Perry and Marla Perry: You guys are true spiritual parents. I love you guys and thank you for teaching me the Word of God, for your patience with me and your love. I love you both!

Now, to my family: To my baby sister, Aundrea Brown: Thanks, Sis. For listening to me bring my story to life. And your input. Love you and Kendale, "Ronie."

Raetequa "Sharae" Brown, my middle sister: Thanks for your genuine support in everything and for listening to me and your input as well. Thank you for coming out to support me on my first speaking engagement; I was so happy when I saw you come in . . . I will never forget that and your kind heart. And I hope that I have inspired you to go after your destiny, and I pray that you see that rare beauty that I have seen in you. Love you!

Amari, my homegirl, my niece: You're just six, but baby, you've been here before. I love you, girl. You don't know how much you help Nanee with my confidence and how it's the little stuff that you notice that no one else does. Love you too, Keidyn, even though we have to work on our bond.

Shout out to my other sister Kristi (Kirvin) and my nieces, Princess, Diamond, Keaoni and Lucy: I love you, guys! Kristi, thank you so much for doing my hair for the cover of my book . . . Honey, you have skills and a God-given talent. Thank you . . . I love you!

Christal Fewell: Thanks for your advice on how I should walk in confidence, no matter what.

Sir Mark Anthony: Godmama loves you!

Maurice Tyler: You have also taught me to believe. Your business mind rubbed off on me and you planted this seed in me and made me believe things I never thought were possible for me. Thank you. Love you, bro.

Keisha Webster: If it weren't for you, I wouldn't have even thought about writing again. And even though we didn't co-write, I know you have a testimony to tell and the world should hear it.

Love you, Nana (Deona), Christopher and Olivia: Godmama loves you guys.

Shout out to the Johnson family (Uncle Pat and Auntie Evette): Love y'all. Thanks for your support and love.

Shout out to the Johnson/Fuller family (Felicia, Charles): Love y'all. Thanks for your support and love.

Shout out to the Brown/William family (Uncle Steve and Aunt Kim): Love y'all. Thank you for your support and love.

Granddaddy (Joel): I love you.

Devin Brown

To my PaPa (Joe): Love you. R.I.P

Courtney (Jessica) Jackson: Girl, you know you were/are my number one fan. Since we were kids you recognized this gift of writing and wanted to hear my made-up stories. I also wanted to thank you in front of the whole wide world for buying my class ring (2002) and allowing me to put my granny's birthstone in it in her memory when I didn't have the money to get it. Most of all, thank you for "the talk" and helping me get through the hardest time in my life. Thank you. Oh, yes, and thanks for creating the name DevinE.

Maya/Steve: Thank you guys for letting for me hang out with you. You have never made me feel like a third wheel. One day I will have a "friend" and we can all double date.

Kesha A. Booth: Girl, you have been there for me when I was going through it with my mother. Thanks for the offer on the iron. Much love, girl.

Kanisha Franklin: Thanks for the talks and prayers. Love you, girl!

Loria Jones: Thank you for all of your advice and encouragements you have shown and given me; I'm so grateful we crossed paths.

Gaye Grossi: Just wanted to thank you for planting a seed in me when it came to corporate America. I look up to you in so many ways. Thank you for the help in the speeches and the talks over lunch.

And to my father, David: I pray that our future continues together and that we grow and love each other unconditionally.

Also to Pastor Tasby and First Lady Arlene Tasby: You guys were my first spiritual parents and have taught me a lot growing up. I just want to let you know that I appreciate you guys for everything and that I love you! Pastor Tasby you have always had a part in my life as a father, thank you!

To Olubukola Olaloko and Adedayo Anucha: Thank you so much for accepting my family. You are so sweet, and you guys know we are so grateful for fixing us FUFU.

Devin Brown

To Briana Pierrelouis I know we don't talk much but I just want to thank you for being a part of my life during the most crucial time in making one of the biggest decisions of my life. I appreciate you being here from every question and concern I had, I never heard you mumble or complain. Thank you!

To Amanda (Mandy) Hall thanks for the many talks and listening hear and for your help with my fundraisers . . . this is your shout out (smile)

To Kinesha Wyatt thank you for all your support and input with the "Aftermath" of my book.

Also a special thanks to Andre` Beverly Sr. Thanks for your help on building my website.

To Debra Jackson (Ms. Debbie) you know you are my girl, I just wanted to say thank you so much for being here there for me, when I had nowhere to go. You embraced me and gave me a place to stay and meals to eat. I will be forever grateful to you. I LOVE YOU MZ.DEBBIE.

To Zundra D'Ann Bateaste—Sutton and Dallas Sutton I want to thank you guys for your constant help and support in helping me get my book off the ground! I am so grateful we cross paths . . . Thank You!

I also want to give a special thanks to "a dude they call Frank": I really do appreciate the unconditional love you have for me and the friendship we contain. Thank you so much for your support you have given me throughout the years. Your words of inspiration and encouragement have helped me in pursuing my dreams. For that I really do appreciate you—you are truly God sent, and I love how you always encourage me to be my own beautiful. Thank you and I love you!

A special thanks to those who helped me raise money by either donating money or participating in the fundraisers.

Also, thanks to the guys that gave their honest opinions in the interviews.

If I have missed anyone, please charge it to my mind not my heart. I love you!

Special thanks to my future fans: Thank you for all your support on my very first book. This could not have been possible with you guys.

Giving Back

I wanted to give back to those who have helped me (my team) on the B.Y.O.B. project. Anybody that loves the work of B.Y.O.B., please feel free to contact my team at:

Eric and Destiny McGill (photographer and makeup artist) at www. blusuedephotography.com and be on the lookout for WHIP LASH.

Also if you like my earrings (the gold ones) contact the designer, Craynetheia Harry.

Company name—Khamilian Designz
Facebook page—KhamilianDesignz ByCraynetheia
instagram—@khamiliandesignz
website—www.etsy.com/shop/KhamilianDesignz
email—khamiliandesignz@gmail.com
KhamilianDesignz—www.etsy.com
Editor—Anne Victory—www.victoryediting.com
Stephanie Long—www.eclecticnistas.bigcartel.com
Cherise Riley—www.DestinyEmpowerment.com
www.twitter.com/DEPROJECT
Pastor Porter L. Perry and First lady Marla Perry—www.**topcf.org**

IT WAS NICE MEETING YOU.

To: _____
    _____

X _____
    _____

(Picture Here)

Devin Brown

Be Your Own Beautiful; by becoming a healthier you. Check Out my Maximum Slim website and our 100% all natural products today to help you reach your healthy goals. (I.E. Weight loss, weight maintenance, lowering high blood pressure, stabilizing blood sugar and so much more).

Check out the website at www.Maximumslim/BeAHealthyYou

With regular exercise this product can help you control your weight, reduce your risk of heart disease, and strengthen your bones and muscles. But before trying this product and if you haven't exercised for some time and you have health concerns, you may want to talk to your doctor before starting a new exercise/health routine. Must be 18 years or older.

Notes

Notes

Notes

Notes

Notes

Notes

Notes